IRAN
IN REVOLT

REVOLUTIONARY ASPIRATIONS

IN A POST-DEMOCRATIC WORLD

HAMID DABASHI

Chicago, Illinois
Haymarket Books

Published in 2025 by
Haymarket Books
P.O. Box 180165
Chicago, IL 60618
www.haymarketbooks.org

ISBN: 9798888902660

Distributed to the trade in the US through Consortium Book Sales and Distribution (www.cbsd.com) and internationally through Ingram Publisher Services International (www.ingramcontent.com).

This book was published with the generous support of Lannan Foundation, Wallace Action Fund, and Marguerite Casey Foundation.

Special discounts are available for bulk purchases by organizations and institutions. Please email info@haymarketbooks.org for more information.

Cover artwork by Arash Mirhadi.
Cover design by Jamie Kerry.

Library of Congress Cataloging-in-Publication data is available.

Entered into digital printing December, 2024.

10 9 8 7 6 5 4 3 2 1

For Farhad Arshad

CONTENTS

INTRODUCTION

WHAT IF "DEMOCRACY" WAS IN BAD FAITH?

*Well, I say this: before one can even begin to apprehend
the reality of our societies, it's necessary, as a preliminary
exercise, to dislodge their emblem. The only way to make
truth out of the world we're living in is to dispel the aura
of the word democracy and assume the burden of not
being a democrat and so being heartily disapproved of by
"everyone" (tout le monde).*

—**Alain Badiou** (2009)

I began my academic career in the late 1970s, mesmerized by the
Iranian Revolution of 1977 to 1979. Decades later, I published
a book on the Arab revolutions of 2009. That trajectory covers
almost half a century of reflecting on the point or use or lasting
consequences of all these revolutions, not just in Iran or the Arab
and Muslim worlds, but the French in the eighteenth century, the
Russian in the twentieth, the Chinese, the Cuban, the Algerian
revolutions that have very much defined the terms of our critical

1

thinking on massive social uprisings. What have we achieved, what have we lost, where do we stand now, decades and generations after so many uprisings and so many upheavals? What constitutes the success of revolutions, and in what terms do we measure their failures? From one end of the Arab and Muslim world to the other, our societies and polities are ruled by military juntas, unelected monarchs, fake and flimsy claims on "democracy," and, above all, millions of defiant people tired of their failed attempts at democratic representations.

All of these reflections percolated in the fall of 2022 when my homeland was once again revolting against an Islamic Republic that has terrorized it for nearly half a century. Was this one among countless other uprisings, soon to be brutally suppressed? Or was it a "real" revolution? To topple the ruling regime and bring to power, what, exactly—the expat monarchists, the cultic Mujaheddin-e Khalq organization, the militant "secularists," as they call themselves, the regime changers funded by an assortment of reactionary venues operating within the US government? And to achieve precisely what? Democracy, rule of law, economic and social justice? Is it possible to entertain such ideals and aspirations any longer, this far into the twenty-first century? I had no doubt about the legitimacy and the justice of the massive uprising in Iran, but how could we trust in meaningful reform internal to the recalcitrant Islamic Republic, or in the assortment of proto-fascist monarchists, secularists, or US-allied regime changers who were clamoring to succeed it?

I had just started graduate school at the University of Pennsylvania in Philadelphia when the Iranian Revolution of 1977 to 1979 began. The American diplomatic corps was taken hostage in Tehran between November 1979 and January 1981. Along with thousands of other Iranian students, I was stranded in the United States and could not go back to Iran to continue my participation in the Iranian Revolution, on which I was planning to write my doctoral dissertation. Therefore, I changed the subject of my dissertation and wrote about an entirely theoretical and distant historical event. With *Authority in Islam: From the Rise of Muhammad to the Establishment of the Umayyads* (1989), I sought to figure out the internal dynamics of the inaugural moment of a world religion that has repeatedly haunted history, always with a vengeance. But I could not stay away from the revolution. In my *Theology of Discontent: The Ideological Foundation of the Islamic Revolution in Iran* (1993), I spent a decade producing a detailed account of the Iranian Revolution. When I published one of my most recent books, *The Emperor Is Naked: On the Inevitable Demise of the Nation-State* (2020), I was completely convinced that the entire colonially manufactured unit of the nation-state and the democracies that are supposed to govern them have run their courses and have no institutional legitimacy anymore—reduced to the skeleton of a colonial relic that exists to torment people rather than ease their lives, a source of their economic deprivation and political destitution rather than a mechanism for social welfare. The myth of the postcolonial state, I thought, had long since lost its mystique. But the obvious question had remained—if the unit of the nation-state is epistemically exhausted and useless, as is the mirage of democracy, then what? Where do we go from here? If the momentum we see in Iran in 2022 has indeed a revolutionary potential, what end is it gearing toward—a better state, a more democratic and representative polity? How could we, in the age of Donald Trump, Narendra Modi, Viktor Orbán, and Jair Bolsonaro, or, closer to home, the geopolitics of Ayatollah Khamenei, Abdel Fattah El-Sisi, Recep

Tayyip Erdoğan, and Bashar al-Assad, still sustain any hope in the prospect of a successful revolution or a representative democracy?

I began to closely follow the events in Iran in the fall of 2022 while asking myself where, if anywhere, is a model for democracy? Russians don't live in a democracy, neither do the Chinese nor the North Koreans, nor do they have any claim to be democratic. What do Americans have that the Chinese and the Russians don't? Freedom, they say? Freedom to do what? To elect Trump, a rapist, white supremacist, evangelical Zionist zealot as their proto-fascist president—who turned around and used and abused the very institutions that brought him to power to stage a violent electoral coup? What do the people of countries like Egypt, Iran, or Turkey want then—to proceed with their democratic struggles so one day they can elect an Egyptian or Turkish or Iranian Trump? Or Biden? Why would any decent human being want to have anything to do with that prospect?

I was not alone in raising such serious questions. In a small volume published more than a decade ago, leading European and American philosophers and political theorists—Giorgio Agamben, Alain Badiou, Daniel Bensaïd, Wendy Brown, Jean-Luc Nancy, Jacques Rancière, Kristin Ross, and Slavoj Žižek—asked similar questions and shared similar anxieties.[1] Democracy was and remains in crisis—not just in places like Iran, Egypt, or Syria that have never experienced it, but even at the very presumed heart of white people's historical claims to it in Europe and the United States. If not for a prospect of democracy in a world that lacks any legitimate example of it then for what are these uprisings all dressed up and ready to go? Where, exactly? There is pain, discontent, corruption, tyranny, and abuse all over the world, and Iran has more than its share. But how are these issues going to be addressed and who will address them? The lackluster son of the deposed and deceased Shah of Iran and his coterie of proto-fascist royalists, the leader of Mujaheddin-e Khalq, a cultic organization code named MEK, good-for-nothing hacks funded by the United States and its regional allies?

"A QUIET REVOLUTION"

What, then, is or could be the alternative? There is no alternative, I concluded. The delusion of democracy was a colonial concoction (a world capitalist ruse) that is now exposed for what it is and over and done with—we've hit a wall with pictures of Trump, Modi, Assad, Sisi, Ayatollah Khamenei, Putin, and the rest of them plastered all over it. This is the case unless, like Hannah Arendt, we make a crucial distinction between freedom from tyranny and liberty to choose a different political system. At this point in history, I have therefore concluded, we are far more invested in freedom from tyranny than harboring any conviction or trust in liberty to choose a legitimate alternative state. I am now convinced we are far better off understanding what has tormented us and despising it than hoping to achieve what we wish and what has historically escaped us. But we need to make a crucial amendment to Arendt's position here. This is what she says in *On Revolution*:

> If the ultimate end of revolution was freedom and the constitution of a public space where freedom could appear, the *constitutio libertatis*, then the elementary republics of the wards, the only tangible place where everyone could be free, actually were the end of the great republic whose chief purpose in domestic affairs should

have been to provide the people with such places of freedom and to protect them.[2]

This position of Arendt, as a condition of public happiness, is still very much in the Jeffersonian terms of the formation of a new republic. In our cases, in postcolonial cases, to which Arendt was entirely indifferent, this becomes useful only if we make a distinction between *freedom from* tyranny and *liberty to* be publicly participant and therefore happy. We are therefore far more invested in our liberty to act on the public space and public sphere cultivating our public reason, rather than harboring the illusion of being free to form a democratic state.

What will happen, then, if we altogether give up on such active delusions of attainable democracy—and simply dwell in the moment of freedom from tyranny? A miracle: we are all liberated from the delusion of democracy and stop being implicated in the spectacle of political careerists pretending they will give it to us. If the vulgar European settler colony that has occupied Palestine for over seventy years and calls itself "Israel" is the "only democracy" in the region, if Trump, Modi, Orbán, and Bolsonaro are the crowning achievement of "Western democracies," I believe the world is better off delivered from this nightmare, to have our moral and political imaginations liberated. The next Iranian or any other revolution will therefore "not be televised," as it were, or tweeted, or theorized. For it will not be a revolution for the delusion of a democracy, but a revolution for the fact of a sustained course of delivery from that delusion. The Revolutionary Guards in Iran may stage a coup; a battle of the Pahlavi dynasty might resume with the custodians of the Islamic Republic, one reactionary front against another; Israel or the United States may launch a military strike against Iran and turn everything upside down. But not one of these scenarios will result in anything remotely resembling a democracy. What they will do is keep the nation on its toes to continue to battle the very idea of the state and the charlatanism of those who promise democracy and deliver tyranny. That battle, that open highway of liberation, is the course of our future.

What is therefore happening today is what the distinguished Iran scholar Ali Mirsepassi has called a "quiet revolution,"[3] or what Asef Bayat has called "a revolution without revolutionaries,"[4] predicated on his idea of "post-Islamism" and "life as politics," and in my own version what I have outlined as the end of the myth of the postcolonial state. There is no reasonable premise, therefore, on which to presume or to expect that any democratic outcome will ever emerge from the revolutionary conditions in Iran, any more than it was, say, in Egypt, Syria, Bahrain, or even Tunisia. If so, what will happen to the cry of justice heard from around the world, but more specifically, from Iran? Iranian women refuse mandatory veiling—the policing of their bodies as a simulacrum of state power. They also demand economic opportunities, social freedom, and political participation—all of which the ruling state has either denied them or else abused to its own advantages. How are any of these objectives to be processed and pursued, let alone achieved? Why am I both optimistic about this uprising that Iranians have code-named "Zhina"—in honor of Mahsa Zhina Amini, who died while in police custody, or "Zan, Zendegi, Azadi" (Women, Life, Freedom), as it is more generally known— and yet deeply troubled by the brutal violence of the ruling state, the lurking fascism of the organized monarchists and militant Islamists known as MEK? What will become of this configuration of political joggling? These are the sorts of questions on my mind as I write these lines.

THE FATEFUL SEPTEMBER AND AFTER

Almost everything that mattered in the Zhina uprising happened within the first few weeks of the revolt, soon after Mahsa Zhina Amini's arrest, incarceration, and death. The whirlwind of events began on September 16, 2022, when news broke out that Mahsa Amini, a twenty-two-year-old woman from Saqqez in western Iran, had died while in police custody. She was arrested by the so-called morality police, or Gasht-e Ershad, for presumably not having proper mandatory hijab. Soon after the revolution in 1979, the ruling Islamist regime had decided that a strict control of women's public appearance was ground zero of its legitimacy as a theocracy. Like all totalitarian regimes they wanted to control the exterior as the simulacrum of brainwashing an entire nation. They had miserably failed. Generation after generation, Iranian women from all walks of life had revolted against mandatory veiling. Almost a month after Khomeini had returned to Iran to establish his violent theocracy, a massive demonstration by women had said no to mandatory veiling on March 8, 1979. This battle remains a live one; the day Mahsa Amini died in custody, it once again broke loose.

Mahsa Zhina Amini was almost instantly considered to have been tortured and murdered by the police. The chant "I will kill whoever killed my sister" was heard and widely echoed on the internet. The following day, September 17, during the funeral of Zhina, protests erupted in her hometown of Saqqez and the nearby provincial capital of Sanandaj, clashes ensued with the police, and casualties were reported. Antigovernment slogans were now chanted loud and clear: "Death to Khamenei!" and "Death to Dictator" were high among other similar slogans. This was no mere protest against a tragic death. The insecure government immediately curtailed the internet. The foreign press has almost no presence in Iran, and Iranian journalists, including those who had reported Mahsa Amini's death in custody, were under severe censorship. By September 18, the protests had spread to Tehran, women and girls were burning their scarves and dancing around the bonfires. The scenes were euphoric. "Death to Dictator" was loud and clear.

By September 19, the protests had spread to Rasht and Isfahan, with the same slogans, identical protests against mandatory veiling. The internet was curtailed even more, but it was useless. All it took was one internet-savvy youngster in any gathering taking pictures or short clips and uploading it—virality ensued. The world's attention was now on Iran, especially among the Iranian communities in Europe, Australia, Canada, and the United States. Years of state abuse, deep-rooted corruption, cronyism, and disregard for human decency had deeply angered millions of Iranians in and out of their homeland. Inside Iran, by September 20, at least sixteen of the thirty-one provinces were deeply engaged in public protests against mandatory veiling and against the whole system of oppression of the Islamic Republic. Among these states were Alborz, Azerbaijan, Fars, Gilan, Golestan, Hormozgan, Isfahan, Kerman, Kermanshah, Kurdistan, Mazandaran, Qazvin, Khorasan, and above all Tehran. The security and intelligence apparatus of the regime and its militarized instruments of oppression were in full gear. By September 22, scenes of burning government buildings and setting cars on fire were widely reported. University campuses were a main site of protests; some classes were canceled, some opted for online classes. The propaganda machinery of the state now staged progovernment and pro-hijab demonstrations by families and friends of state employees. It was useless. The protests were not against veiling. They were against mandatory veiling.

The protests were now reported neighborhood by neighborhood, in small cities and major cosmopolises. Small and large demonstrations were blossoming like a sudden spring, as fall yielded to winter. Government officials looked and sounded miserable. By September 26, protests were reported from Tehran, Tabriz, Yazd, Sanandaj, Borazjan, and Karaj. By September 29, antigovernment demonstrations continued in several cities throughout the country. Police, meanwhile, arrested Iranian songwriter Shervin Hajipour, whose viral song "Baraye" (For the Sake of) had gained millions of Instagram views and become the unofficial anthem of the Zhina protests. A key event happened in Zahedan on September 30, when security forces fired on civilians during Friday prayers; at least eighty-two people were reported killed. Amnesty International and Human Rights Watch issued damning reports of human rights abuses committed against people while in custody.

By October 1, worldwide protests were held in solidarity with the uprising in Iran. Demonstrations brandishing the slogan of "Women, Life, Freedom" took place in many major cities, including Auckland, London, Melbourne, New York, Los Angeles, Paris, Ottawa, San Francisco, Montreal, Rome, Seoul, Stockholm, Sydney, and Zurich. On October 3, Supreme Leader Ali Khamenei made his first comments about the protests, blaming Israel and the United States for the upheaval in the country. He then fully endorsed the security forces. On October 22, tens of thousands of Iranians staged a massive demonstration in Berlin against the government and its abuses. The pain and suffering that the misbegotten Islamic Republic had caused millions of Iranians in and out of their homeland was now on full display. The mojahedin were involved in organizing, as were the monarchists, as were ethnic separatists of varied sorts, with perfectly legitimate grievances against the ruling state and yet trapped inside a reactionary ethnic nationalism that would have caused more grief than solace. But at the heart of all these protests, all the nefarious forces integral to them as they were, was the loud and clear cry for freedom from an Islamist republic that had long since overstayed its welcome.

When the World Cup began in Qatar, the Iranian national soccer team was in the spotlight. On November 21, members of the Iranian men's soccer team remained silent while the national anthem played ahead of their match with England. This was perceived as the team distancing itself from the violent government. On December 4, state officials declared that the morality police was abolished—which some considered a small victory for the protests. But by early December, the state publicly hanged a couple of demonstrators convicted of injuring security guards during the protests.

MISREADING THE UPRISING

Since its very inception in the aftermath of the Iranian Revolution, the ruling regime has been accustomed to periodic protests. Throughout its forty-six years in power, there have been regular and major periods of unrest, demonstrating to the world that something was rotten in the Islamic Republic. The Green Movement of the 2000s, the Reform Movement of the 1990s, plus successive student protests, labor unrest, all going back to the first women's uprising against mandatory veiling on March 8, 1979—the history of the Islamic Republic is in fact the history of major components of society questioning its legitimacy. You might even say the Islamic Republic was inoculated against meaningful reform and collapse by being consistently forced to deal with these serious challenges against its rule.

What were these protests for? Initially to correct the course of the 1977 to 1979 revolution and restore its pluralistic forces. Then to reform the regime from inside itself. Finally, they were expressions of the discredited and expat forces—led by the Pahlavi monarchists and the mojahedin—trying to come back with a vengeance. The protests also had multiple Rashomon-effect readings. Was the aim to restore the Pahlavis back to power? Was it to bring the mojahedin back to power? Was it to turn Iran into a satellite state of a US-Israeli-Saudi alliance? Or were all these genuine revolutionary uprisings against all such flawed and abusive readings? Common to all such readings was the fact that a restless young population was sick and tired of an aging clerical tyranny and its praetorian guards, sick and tired of the plundering of national resources in regional adventurism, sick and tired of corrupt elites of the Islamist regime taking the whole country hostage, sick and tired of militant Islamism replicating European Zionism and turning their homeland into a garrison state. Israel and the Islamic Republic may appear as each other's arch enemies, but they are in fact the mirror images of each other—two ideological by-products of European colonialism. Were these uprisings the harbingers of a revolution to end all revolutions? The illusion of a democratic revolution was always there—but never its realistic prospects. This post-Islamist unfolding of state illegitimacy seemed like the end of the very idea of the postcolonial state, and the demise of Islamism as a political project—in short, the beginning of an open-ended revolt for liberty from tyranny rather than freedom to form a more democratic state.

Preventing a full recognition of what these successive uprisings were all about is how the global community, led by the United

States and its allies, consistently misread it—a misreading that the ruling Islamist state encouraged and echoed. Contrary to what the custodians of the Islamist regime were saying, the United States and Israel were not the cause of these protests. Quite the contrary, they were the models for teaching the ruling regime how to suppress and pacify them. The United States and Israel are world leaders in violently suppressing popular uprisings—also known globally by the Palestinian term "Intifada." As the ruling regime in Iran violently cracked down on mostly peaceful demonstrators fed up with a repressive government, the United States imposed new sanctions on Islamist officials. The US media endorsed such sanctions, while in Israel the ruling apartheid regime actively sided with the protesters. But the central question is, why would Israel, or the United States, or Saudi Arabia want to see a free, liberated, and progressive state in Iran, instead of a weak, vulnerable, and bruised Islamist regime with serious legitimacy issues on the home front?

You read the news and you may think how noble and thoughtful of the United States and Israel to lend a helping hand in solidarity to support the otherwise helpless Iranians protesting a vicious and violent regime that, for decades now, has been bereft of any semblance of legitimacy. You may be forgiven for the impression that, at such crucial times, when millions of Iranians were protesting mandatory veiling (never voluntary veiling) and other repressive measures by their reactionary government, it was wonderful to receive such support from a global and a regional superpower. This might all be fine until you realize that the selfsame United States and its main regional settler colony lead by example, not by rhetorical and hypocritical gestures. The United States leads the world in militarizing its police force. This massively militarized police and the sustained record of suppressing peaceful social protest in the United States and among its chief allies are the very models the Islamic Republic of Iran follows closely to maim, murder, and suppress Iranians protesting the ruling regime that has tormented them for over forty years. The Israeli military forces in occupied Palestine are another veritable model that Iranian security and intelligence forces follow closely when violently cracking down on Iranian protesters. Beneath and beyond the rhetoric of the Islamic Republic and its regional and global nemesis dwells a whole different algorithm of undemocratic and violent forces vying for power against all forms of liberation movements—from Ferguson, to Palestine, to Iran.

TROUBLED DEMOCRACIES

We should think of the successive Iranian uprisings as a version of the Palestinian Intifada—what do Israelis do with successive waves of Intifada? They violently suppress them and systematically vilify Palestinians. Well, this is precisely what the Iranian military, security, and intelligence forces do with Iranian protesters engaged in their own version of Intifada, or "Khizesh," as we might suggest its Persian equivalent. The repressive measures and tactics that the Islamists use in Iran have been perfected by the United States, Israel, and in other locations inspired by their exemplary models. Consider, for example, when hundreds of thousands of Canadians protested the G20 Summit in Toronto in June 2010. What did the Canadian police do? With exemplary violence, the Canadian police attacked demonstrators, journalists, and even bystanders as if they were trained by the Basijis in Tehran. In 2013, the International Network of Civil Liberties Organizations published a report about the crackdown on peaceful protests around the world, in which it showed how "the tactics include excessive (sometimes deadly) police force and the criminalization of dissent."[5] What were the leading countries offered as examples in this study? The United States, the UK, Canada, and Israel. Other examples in the report were Egypt, Argentina, South Africa, Kenya, and Hungary, all following the model of "Western democracies." To which we might certainly add Iran. If the world were to be spared their crocodile tears, the United States, the UK, Canada, and their favorite settler colony Israel teach the most reactionary and violent regimes in the world how to suppress dissent. What are we then to think of the spectacle of "democracy"? That these countries democratically elect their representative to teach the world how to violently suppress other people's uprisings to demand democracy? The whole idea is simply obscene.

The United States and Israel are the pioneering innovators in the militarization of policing. In his book *Rise of the Warrior Cop* (2014), the investigative reporter Radley Balko has detailed how, "over the last two centuries, America's cops have increasingly come to resemble ground troops. The consequences have been dire: the home is no longer a place of sanctuary, the Fourth Amendment has been gutted, and police today have been conditioned to see the citizens they serve as enemies."[6] This is precisely, almost word for word, what the ruling regime in Iran does with Iranian citizens.

Where do American militarized police go to train how to maim and murder Americans who, just like Iranians, dare to protest their conditions? They go to the "only democracy in the Middle East," that is, Israel, to train. In a 2016 blog post, Amnesty International detailed how "Baltimore law enforcement officials, along with hundreds of others from Florida, New Jersey, Pennsylvania, California,

Arizona, Connecticut, New York, Massachusetts, North Carolina, Georgia, Washington state as well as the DC Capitol police have all traveled to Israel for training. Thousands of others have received training from Israeli officials here in the US."[7] The United States and Israel combined, with two identical claims on being a "Western democracy," have perfected the art and science of brutalizing people, African Americans in the United States and Palestinians in Palestine, and Iran closely follows their example with its own citizens.

No national liberation movement from domestic tyranny or colonial occupation happens in a vacuum. The Islamic Republic has actively woven itself into the geopolitics of the region, from Yemen to Afghanistan, to Syria, Lebanon, Palestine, and now even Ukraine. For all their loud protestations against each other, the United States, Israel, Saudi Arabia, and the ruling regime in Iran are remarkably similar in their treatment of innocent and defenseless people at the mercy of their systematic cruelties. What we are witnessing in Iran is a grassroots revolt against endemic tyranny and unbridled cruelty and corruption of the ruling state. Iranian women of all walks of life are leading this uprising. If these Iranians have any friends around the world in this struggle, they are not in the halls of power in Tel Aviv, London, or Washington, DC. Their support and solidarity comes entirely from the communities who are the victims of these violent states: Black and other minorities at the mercy of police brutalities in the United States, Palestinians in their occupied homeland, the brutalized people in Afghanistan and Iraq bearing the scars of US invasions and occupations of their homelands. The vulnerable lives and fragile liberties of nations have never been so intimately connected with each other as they are today, just as the pernicious cruelties of the ruling regimes tormenting them have never been so identical as they are today in the United States, Israel, Saudi Arabia, Egypt, Syria, and Iran. All in one breath.

The question of which one of these countries has a claim to democracy and which one does not becomes entirely irrelevant in their collective constitution of a total state in charge of a killing apparatus ruling over identically naked lives. For much of the world at the receiving end of Eurocentric politics of domination, democracy has always already been in bad faith. What is happening in Iran today is the harbinger of a post-democratic world where, liberated from the delusion of any just state, we are cultivating the prospect of a just society.

ONE

REVOLUTIONARY ASPIRATIONS IN A POST-DEMOCRATIC WORLD

If we were to ask if the Zhina event and its aftermath is a revolution, I believe that this is not the beginning of a revolution but the external manifestations of a revolution that has gradually taken place for the last two decades in people's mindset, in their form of living, and in their social relations. The only revolutionary aspect of this uprising is that people wish for this change also to be recognized at the street level too and a confession to be made that the revolution has already happened.

—**Mohammad Haqmoradi** (November 2022)

The Zhina uprising is forcing us all to reexamine most of our assumptions about the very idea of a "revolution." For some: yes, this is a revolutionary moment but in what particular terms? For others: no, this is not a revolution in the classic sense of the term but something perhaps more important. What exactly is it then? Over the last year a number of cogent critical assessments have emerged, thinking perhaps too enthusiastically through the implications of the Zhina uprising. Common to most of these writings is the sense that despite its similarities to many other previous uprisings, there is a uniqueness to this event, which should not be assimilated backward to what we already know about other similar world historic events. But what exactly are those features? Among the most fanatical forces, bordering with fascism, but very much limited to the cyberplace, are the Pahlavi monarchists who have come out of the woodwork, as it were, declaring that the Iranian Revolution of 1977 to 1979 was in fact a terrible riot gone wrong, that we should all rush to go back to the Pahlavi monarchy and resume our lives after forty-odd years of rude interruptions. But the realities on the ground, which more serious scholars and critical thinkers have sought to understand, speak of a different dynamic at work defining this insurrectionary moment. We need to remain cautious of the Pahlavi monarchist, particularly considering the possibility of how the United States and its regional allies might put them to work for their own nefarious purposes. Yet understanding the dynamics of the uprising cannot be limited to these varied pathologies.

"A REVOLUTIONARY CONFUSION"?

"Sargijeh-ye Enqelabi-ye Asef Bayat" (The Revolutionary Confusion of Asef Bayat) reads the title of a critical essay on the distinguished Iranian sociologist Asef Bayat and the manner in which over the years he has sought to explain various revolutionary

uprisings in the Arab and Muslim world, including his initial
assessments of the Zhina uprising.[1] The author of this critical
essay, Saman Safarza'i, feels triumphant for having caught Bayat's
"confusions" about the revolutionary uprisings he has sought to
understand—musing on whether or not they are revolutionary,
and, if so, in what particular terms. The author begins this essay
with Bayat's observations back in 2018 when he was discussing his
book *Revolution without Revolutionaries,* in which he tries to make
sense of the Arab Spring.[2] Saman Safarza'i, who is evidently quite
ill-informed about the Arab world (he names the world-renowned
Egyptian revolutionary Sayyid Qotb as "Sa'id Qotb"), describes
Bayat's book as a comparative assessment of the 1970s revolutions, which he says were rooted in an ideology, as opposed to the
events of the Arab Spring, which he says have no such anchor. The
author's point here is to find contradictions and confusions on the
part of Bayat, comparing and contrasting his evolving positions on
the Arab Spring, and with that the very idea of revolution.

By way of demonstration, the author lists all the horrors that
have happened in the Arab world since the Arab Spring—mass
incarcerations in Egypt, mass murder in Syria, famine in Yemen,
and other atrocities, in Libya in particular. He lists these atrocities
as if they were all the fault of a sociologist trying to make sense of
a revolutionary uprising in the Arab world. While criticizing Bayat
for what he believes to be "a fetish with revolution," Mr. Safarza'i
seems to be entirely oblivious to his coming across as a sordidly
reactionary defender of the status quo. At the end, the author falls
flat into the abyss of reactionary submission to things as they are.
Yes, citing some of the disasters that have occurred in the aftermath of both the Iranian Revolution of 1977 to 1979 and the Arab
revolutions of 2010 are facts and even truisms, but thereby positing

a flat-footed defense of the astoundingly reactionary assessment is also a by-product of that very calamity. Bayat's constant efforts are not a "fetish with revolution" at all. Quite the contrary. He is one of the most insightful, patient, and persistent contemporary theorists of collective behavior trying to understand what is happening in the course of these uprisings. Pinning the criminal atrocities of the Arab revolution on Bayat's presumed "fetishism" with revolution is too silly to be taken seriously. What the piece does offer, however, is the site of a reactionary force today at the heart of the Iranian society—a reactionary position that inevitably yearns for a return of the Pahlavis.

Let us take a look at one of the most insightful recent works of Asef Bayat, *Life as Politics: How Ordinary People Change the Middle East* (2010), where he proposes a novel and pathbreaking way of looking at popular uprisings in and out of the Arab world. In this book, Bayat altogether changes our perception of revolution by remapping the course of its operation from a sudden epic event to a gradual unfolding into what in my own book on the Arab revolution I have compared with the course of a novel. Bayat's book was and remains prophetic in its manner of making us think about revolutions, enabling us to rethink social and political agency and new special spaces. Consider his assessment of the condition of women in the Arab and Muslim world: "Under the authoritarian patriarchal states, whether secular or religious, women's activism for gender equality is likely to take on the form of non-movement"—meaning becoming endemic and translucent rather than bombastic and disruptive.[3] This kind of thinking is chiefly responsible for our shifting perceptions of what movements such as the Zhina uprising mean and signify. Of course, one can understand the cause of the fearful reactionary politics of Saman Safarza'i. This is a generation that has suffered the consequences of an Islamic theocracy wrongly conflating that suffering and the militant Islamism that has caused it with the revolutionary momentum of the 1970s. The Zhina uprising, however, should neither be assimilated backward to the events of the 1970s nor taken as so entirely unique that it cannot be subjected to comparative assessments that scholars like Asef Bayat represent.

"REVOLUTION HAS ALREADY HAPPENED"

It is impossible to understand the nature and disposition of the Zhina uprising without paying close attention to how Iranians on the ground read and come to terms with it. Social scientists of different disciplines, economists, sociologists, journalists, students of mass movements, and political activists have all written on the various dimensions of the uprising since day one. These writings are by far the most valuable body of literature produced on the Zhina uprising. There is a jarring disconnect between how Iranians writing in Persian understand this uprising in their grounded and learned essays and the delusional politics of mass frenzy caused by a handful of so-called celebrities from outside Iran with their vacuous speculations on social media.

A key issue for Iranians, as we saw in the case of Asef Bayat, is the specific ways in which we might consider this uprising a revolution. In short: What is it we are witnessing? In an essay dated November 28, 2022, for *Naqd-e Eqtesad-e Siasi* (Critique of Political Economy), a leading critical online journal, Mohammad Haqmoradi develops what he calls a "non-ideology" for the Zan, Zendegi, Azadi uprising.[4] In this essay the author considers the contradictions of "modernity" as the condition of current political despairs. He traces the Zhina uprising back to the very origin of the idea of the nation-state, where issues such as the rule of law, women's rights, or progress began to define our historical circumstances. What is happening today, Haqmoradi believes, is not just an "excessive accumulation" of youth, but also of hopes, dreams, aspirations. He believes the dominant ideology of the ruling state is in dire need of reproducing itself, but he is fully aware that it is not working and therefore is happy even with a formal respect for it, while contemporary movements are fleeting without a program, leaders, and organization. The point of such protest is the protest itself, so that the ruling regime knows people are protesting and that they can protest. He then asserts:

> If we were to ask if the Zhina event and its aftermath is a revolution, I believe that this is not the beginning of a revolution but the external manifestations of a revolution that has gradually taken place for the last two decades in people's mindset, in their form of living, and in their social relations. The only revolutionary aspect of this uprising is that people wish for this change also to be recognized at the street level too and a confession to be made that the revolution has already happened.[5]

With a population of about eighty-five million, Iran is a youthful country; the infant mortality rate has sharply fallen over the last century. Trying in vain to control this youthful population, the ruling Islamist regime utilizes a massive military, security, and intelligence apparatus that spreads from inside the country itself and widely into the region, as far as Yemen in the south and Ukraine in the north. It has woven itself into strategic alliances with Russia and China, and if need be it will happily cooperate with the United States and EU to keep itself in power. There is very little short of a massive armed rebellion or foreign military intervention that can shake this garrison state—and even those drastic measures will not dismantle it. Either of those two scenarios will turn the state into a more militarized garrison completely severed from the population. Much of these speculations about "quiet revolutions" or "open-ended revolutions" or revolutions that have already happened are desperate desires for a fundamental change in the status quo that may or may never happen. In short, the Zhina uprising is a reality in search of a reading, of an interpretation, of a theory—and so far there is no such grand narrative that might define this uprising in fully convincing ways.

But why is that the case?

"FOOTLOOSE DEMOCRACY"

What do the millions of Iranians pouring into their streets, alleys, squares, and social media pages want? An end to this Islamic Republic, for sure. But what else? The Pahlavi monarchists believe and scream loudly that they want the monarchy back. Some Iranians no doubt do, with a profound sense of nostalgia, especially after more than four decades of a wretched theocracy. But can we extend that sentiment to a mighty political force to dismantle the Islamic Republic? I seriously doubt that. Reza Pahlavi and his mother the former queen seem to hope that the Revolutionary Guards will stage a military coup and bring them back to power. This is a delusional pipe dream. If the Revolutionary Guards did stage a coup it would be to protect their own vastly invested interests—now camouflaged by an octogenarian fraternity club of frazzled clerics. Why would they want to bring back the son of a deposed monarch some forty years after their demise?

Be that as it is, the public cry in the street for "Azadi," or freedom, is the defining moment of the uprising: "Zan, Zendegi, Azadi." But freedom from what? Freedom from tyranny for sure, and perforce for democracy. But is democracy still plausible? Let us pull back a bit and look at the more global condition of the thing that calls itself democracy. "Democracy has historically unparalleled global popularity today yet has never been more conceptually footloose or substantively hollow."[6] Wendy Brown's cogent assessment is not just theoretically sound, but also founded in our global lived experiences of the last two hundred years. She compares the word "democracy" to the former US president Barack Obama, "an empty signifier to which any and all can attach their dreams and hopes."[7] But why would any sane person want to chase after an empty signifier—Obama or democracy—and invest in it undeserving hopes? Obama was a miserable career opportunist who banked on his father's race and his mother's faith to carve himself a lucrative niche in the heart of a brutalized people. He made his millions and, like any other charlatan, ran away to his private life. He is over and done with and lives in the lap of luxury. Perhaps it is the same with the word "democracy." If the mass murdering machine of BJP in India and the settler colonialism of Israel represent democracies, why value this "empty signifier"—which in fact does not look quite empty but is filled with the horror stories of our time.

Brown says capitalism is "the nonidentical twin of democracy," which has now reduced it to a brand, "a late modern twist on commodity fetishism that wholly severs a product's salable image from its content."[8] Fine analogy, but too late for the rest of us at the colonial edges of that selfsame capitalism to entertain such conscious awareness of commodity fetishism. We are no longer fooled into buying this brand, and at its pernicious colonial edges, capitalism could not sustain any such delusion for democracy. It is by now clear that the idea of democracy was always a sham, a mirage used by global capitalism to pacify any mode of resistance to it. Brown is therefore wrong to think democracy is popular today.[9] It is not. Its terrorizing prospects are all over the world. Democracy is a racist premise for the rise of fascism of the most pernicious sort. American democracy in particular is an existential threat to world peace. How many Trumps can the world take? How many even "smarter" Trumps are still in the offing? What frightens people like Brown— the "securitization" of the state apparatus—has been the story of our lives around the globe under surveillance of European colonialism, which has now come home to roost. Philosophers like Brown are free to question if humans really want freedom over safety and comfort.[10] But for the rest of the world freedom is not a philosophical luxury. It is a matter of survival. Freedom, not in the abstract sense of "liberté, égalité, fraternité," but freedom within the limited parameters of modest voluntary associations of labor unions, student assemblies, and women's rights organizations to protect their livelihood and dignities against the monstrosities of all postcolonial polities, rentier states, and unleashed pure violence—above all, against the delusion of democracy.

"WE ARE MARXISTS!"

"We are Marxists. We are not neutral. We are on the side of the oppressed. We are committed to the revolution. We are irreconcilable with tyranny and imperialism. One can cross the desert without a pair of shoes—but not without a guiding star."

These staccato sentences are on the top of an Instagram account called "The Voice of Black Fish" that, soon after the commencement of the Zhina uprising in fall 2022, popped up on a list of suggested sites to follow. I called a trusted leftist friend in Berlin, a revolutionary activist jailed under the ruling Islamist regime multiple times, and asked if she knew who was behind "Black Fish." Without missing a beat she said, "I think they are the Aqaliyyat, though I am not quite sure." The Aqaliyyat here refers to a minority faction of the Marxist revolutionaries of Cherik-ha-ye Fada'i-e Khalq Organization, or the Organization of People's Devotees, that refused to compromise with Khomeini's abduction of the Iranian Revolution. Another graduate student from northern Iran, however, said these were a group of leftist activists based inside Iran. There were a few other accounts like "Voice of Black Fish" that were tirelessly active on social media, posting mainly in Persian but also occasionally in German, English, French, or Spanish. The most caring, competent, and invested faction of the activists on the ground and in cyberspace were in conversation with them. From the commencement of the Zhina uprising I was following these accounts closely, as was a platoon of Pahlavi fanatics that had suddenly flooded cyberspace. And saner and more balanced pages too.

"I can't believe you are supporting this movement. Can't you see Americans, Israelis, and the Saudis are all behind it?"

This statement: almost verbatim from a close progressive Arab friend who could not come to terms with an uprising that had the active support of the monarchists, the Mujaheddin-e Khalq, the US "regime changers," and Saudi enemies of the ruling Islamic

Republic. Add to this list websites of colorful characters, BBC Persian, handsome Hollywood actors, and more, who were pushing for a regime change, each following their own political agenda or getting involved in the hype. How could I, as the Arab friend put it, support such a movement?

From the left of the left to the right of the right, many were actively opposing the ruling Islamist regime. What could an independent critical stand be? Those who were active on behalf of the uprising on the left had little to no funding, which they compensated with steadfast conviction and relentless work. The progressive left who were following the events unfold closely had every reason to trust and invest in this uprising, because their perceptions were deeply local, informed by subaltern forces in the most poverty-stricken parts of the country, in Baluchistan, Kurdistan, Lorestan, or Khuzestan. While the world media had a very jaundiced reading of the events unfolding, so too did the progressive left around the world, out of touch with facts on the ground and at the mercy of the media they would ordinarily mistrust. The very same progressive left on the fringes of the events have every reason to be suspicious of the notorious right-wing neoliberal regime-changers based in the United States and their animated enthusiasm to twist it to their own benefit. But what exactly is their benefit? Here the position of United States, Israel, or Saudi Arabia is not exactly to topple this regime but to weaken it and make it more subservient to their will. But what about the Iranian people and their legitimate grievances against a deeply corrupt and morally compromised ruling state?

From the outside the leading slogan of the uprising, "Women, Life, Freedom," was replete with evident paradoxes. It celebrated women but basked in misogynistic curses targeting their opponents' mothers and sisters, it celebrated life but championed a man, Mohammad Moradi, who, on December 26, 2022, committed suicide in Lyon, France, to protest the atrocities of the Islamic Republic. It celebrated freedom but included the most vicious attacks on any political enemy with the slightest divergence from the monarchists' point of view. The movement as a movement was both historical and ahistorical, rooted in modern Iranian history and yet quite unique in its nature and disposition. Still, at the core of it, there remained a force that demanded critical attention. The central issue, the primary impetus that must remain at the heart of our understanding of this uprising, is the woman's body, which has been a central cause of anxiety for the masculinist patriarchy ruling over the land for millennia, irrespective of dynasties or dubious claims to being a republic. Women's bodies here point to the body-politics—and the proverbial formula of the king having two bodies but no clothes. From Reza Shah to his son Mohammad Reza Shah, and now their current progeny Reza Pahlavi, a particular figure of European-looking woman was propagated as definitive to their politics. The ruling Islamist ideologues had sought in vain to institutionalize and make normative a different conception of a "pious" woman. Both these figures were historically manufactured and yet had their respective constituencies. But they had both also become definitive to an ideological foregrounding of the polity they envisioned and embodied. The critical left, more a voice and a vision rather than a political party, kept pushing for the freedom of choice and the centrality of women as key decision-makers.

Under this conflicting cacophony of voices and forces, in what particular sense do I suggest we consider this uprising "post-democratic"? There is a strong fascistic impatience agitating under the skin of this movement, and it will rear its ugly head the instant the Islamic Republic falls—or even appears to be falling. The real, enduring struggle will start the day after the Islamic Republic falls. The monarchists, MEK, and the coterie of regime changers in the United States, Canada, and EU are the main forces of this lurking fascism. They have enormous power and a massive unpaid army. The real struggle of workers, women, and students will start after the fall of the Islamic Republic, when they face an evolving fascism. The sacrifices of people from all walks of life are being confiscated by expat monarchists in Los Angeles (putting the sign of Mahsa Amini and Zan, Zendegi, Azadi on their Lamborghinis). If this is to be a lasting revolution and not a monarchic fascism chasing after an Islamist theocracy, we need to think of it in successive waves. We are now facing both the monarchists who seek to regain what they lost in 1979 and the Islamists holding fast to the power that they hijacked in the Iranian Revolution of 1977 to 1979. What we are witnessing is not the real event—this is the fake event. The focus must therefore remain solidly on poverty-stricken spots like Kurdistan, Baluchistan, Lorestan, Khuzestan, and Azerbaijan, where the grassroots labor, women, and student organizations are the seeds of the real revolution. We should not be distracted by the surface war between two reactionary forces and their trolls crowding the internet—as the Saudis and the Israelis, as well as European and US right-wing politicians, act as cheerleaders for these reactionary forces.

The key question today, as this movement unfolds to unforeseen conclusions, is how should the left in both the global north and in the global south (perhaps itself a false binary) understand such uprisings in the context of national and transnational histories—to be supportive or suspicious of them? What, in other words, are the pitfalls that we should avoid when making sense of what is happening in Iran? For these and other similar reasons we need to have a clear conception of the demands being articulated in this particular moment. Equally crucial is no longer to fall into the false and outdated East-West binary, while keeping in mind the role of the United States and UK at previous historical junctures, while at the same time allowing such traumatic moments to inform the world of the terms of their own articulations. We must therefore begin with a sweeping consciousness at the outset before we focus on the class and social dynamics at play in this uprising, with particular attention to arts and literature that have foregrounded such uprisings in specific terms. I began actively and closely following this movement almost from the day it started in mid-September 2022, and it was not until six months into the unfolding events in mid-March 2023 that I had a better grasp of its pitfalls and promises. What I write, therefore, is based on my lifetime reflections on such uprisings and yet with attention to the dynamics at work in this specific moment—where we do not have any formal and organized left political party, but when critical thinking is interwoven into the very fabric of our political judgments.

In this historicization, we ought to be careful to guard against obsessive historicism. We must allow for history to inform us but not to assimilate this uprising backward to what we already know. We must allow for the specifics of this moment to articulate itself. For one thing, I am absolutely convinced that no democratic state of any sort will emerge from this uprising. If the Islamic Republic falls (which would be good), an equally or even worse tyranny will emerge (which would be no good). This does not mean people must put a stop on their revolutionary enthusiasm, but that it must be directed toward far more detailed democratic intuitions at local and grassroots levels rather than in the grand illusion of a democratic state of one brand or another.

From the iconic events of the Constitutional Revolution of the early 1900s, to the tumultuous decade of the 1910s, we eventually reach the 1920s, when Reza Khan, aided and abetted by the British, stages a coup that eventually leads to the Allied occupation of Iran in the 1930s and the formation of the leftist Tudeh Party in the 1940s. Soon after that, in the 1950s, the Iranian oil industry is nationalized, and this is then aborted by the military coup of 1953 that was engineered by the United States and Britain. This leads to two decades of ironfisted Pahlavi rule in the 1950s and 1960s, which is in turn interrupted by the Khomeini-led revolt in 1963 and the guerrilla uprising of Siahkal in 1971, which then paves the way for the revolution of 1977 to 1979. The success of the Iranian Revolution in the late 1970s was, therefore, contingent on the three successive uprisings of the 1950s marked by anticolonial nationalism of Mosaddegh, the militant Islamism of the 1960s led by Ayatollah Khomeini, and the Marxist guerrilla uprisings of the early 1970s. The same dynamic that resulted in the violent formation of the Islamic Republic in 1979 would be followed, after its consolidation, by the hostage crisis of 1979 to 1981, the Iran-Iraq War of 1980 to 1988, followed by the Reformist Movement of the 1990s, and the Green Movement of the 2000s. The Green Movement was severely crushed and began to resurrect in various uprisings that ultimately crescendoed in 2022 with the Zhina uprising. This is a short history of the Iranian revolutionary disposition of the last century that must inform our reading of this and any other uprising but not reduce them to just one leitmotif.

POST-ISLAMIST LIBERALISM:
"THIS GOVERNMENT MUST GO!"

Critical thinking against the ruling Islamist regime, however, has equally potent liberal voices. Bahareh Hedayat (born 1981) is an Iranian political and women's rights activist who became famous when she joined other women's rights activists working on the One Million Signatures campaign to change laws that discriminate against women in Iran. The One Million Signatures campaign was active between 2006 and 2013 and became a major social manifestation of the changing demographics of women's rights in the country. The campaign was the most ambitious women's and civil rights project focusing on the status of women in the Islamic Republic. Among the leading advocates of this campaign were Nobel Peace Prize winner Shirin Ebadi; the late prominent poet Simin Behbahani; scholar, publisher, and activist Shahla Lahiji; poet Babak Ahmadi; the late Marxist economist Fariborz Raisdana; and scores of other prominent activists. The campaigners were emphatic that their demands were not contrary to Islam. The campaign had received much acclaim and recognition around the world. The violent and reactionary factions of the ruling regime, however, ultimately dismantled the campaign.

Bahareh Hedayat began her political activities when she was still a student and a member of the Dafter-e Tahkim-e Vahdat, or the Office of Consolidating Unity, a nationwide student organization that the ruling regime ultimately infiltrated, destroying its progressive potential and appropriating the organization into its own reactionary forces. Because of her political activities in this and other movements Hedayat has been repeatedly arrested and jailed. She was last arrested for protesting the downing of the

Ukrainian airliner on January 8, 2020, when 176 passengers and crew members were killed. Soon after the Zhina uprising began in September 2022 she wrote a letter from jail that was widely circulated, read, and discussed. In this letter, Hedayat declared:

> The essence and destiny of this government is darkness and it must go. Dismantling this criminal state will no doubt be costly and dangerous. But there is no other way than accepting these costs and facing such dangers—for the structure of this state does not have the capacity to digest and recognize the legitimacy of modern social forces.[11]

A close reading of this letter is a window into the political mind of a principled revolutionary activist deeply committed to progressive liberal aspirations. The letter begins with her expression of anger and frustration about the Zhina uprising, when young protesters were beaten, tortured, and even hanged. She believes the ruling Islamist region is incapable of reform, for it is constitutionally dark and diabolic, and it must be dismantled. The revolution is therefore inevitable. She is worried about the cycle of violence and warns against it—though she thinks it inevitable. She considers her generation, the Daheh Shasti-ha, or the 1980ers, as those who had the last chance for peaceful reform, which the ruling regime made impossible. She regrets that the Green Movement of 2009 and 2010 was too conciliatory toward the ruling regime. She now considers the Reformists led by President Khatami (but eventually including Mir Hossein Mousavi) as having lost the momentum of the movement. The Reformists triumphed in giving a Reformist reading to the Green Movement, despite its far more radical potential. With the Green Movement, she believes that "Islam-e Siasi" (political Islam) also ended. She bitterly denounces Mir Hossein Mousavi for hav-

ing called the founder of the Islamic Republic Ayatollah Khomeini
"Jan-e Bidar" (the Living Soul). There were two radically opposed
conceptions of reform, she suggests: one that meant to keep the
regime alive, and the other seeking far more radical reforms done
peacefully. She had advocated for the latter. The Zhina uprising is
now devoid of the traces of that political Islam, she believes, and
has no religious dimension, and is intent on dismantling the regime
once and for all.

Hedayat then turns to the question of mandatory veiling or
hijab and writes that, by burning their scarves, Iranian women
have put "the West" (which she uses as a legitimate and appropriate
category without the slightest sense of critical concerns) on notice
that hijab is not a cultural matter, and their attempt to normalize
hijab is wrong. Such reading of the hijab is specific to "the West"
and has nothing to do with Iran. Then comes the real contention:

> This movement [to normalize hijab] that occasionally
> even calls itself anticolonial, in fact harbors an entirely
> colonial attitude and puts its fingers into its ears when
> the Muslim-born Middle Eastern women speak against
> hijab, and calls us who are living inside the situation from
> outside the situation "Islamophobic"! In other words, I as
> a woman from the Middle East am not allowed even to
> protest against the subaltern constitution of hijab based
> on so-called progressive principles issued from the West
> and its intellectual circles. This protest against the his-
> torical injustice that Islam has imposed on me is consid-
> ered "Islamophobic," and no one is allowed to be afraid
> of Islam, because the Western intellectual faces the bar-
> riers of assimilation of Muslims into their societies, and
> because it has fallen into the stupor of Islamist fundamen-

talism, and because it cannot believe the phenomenon of hijab has the potential of creating a chain of repression, subalternity, and alienation, without having any evident link to capitalism, and because it is addicted to seeing everything from the vantage point of capitalism, then the circle of its understanding cannot go beyond it, it does not give the Middle Eastern woman even the right to protest so that its own intellectual tensions are exposed. The 1401 (2022) protest began by burning the scarves and suddenly called on all those pseudo-intellectual trends to pay attention to realities.[12]

She turns to the issue of ethnic minorities, suggesting that this uprising might be the beginning of a new covenant among them. She finally turns to Immanuel Kant for having presumably said that experiences without ideas are blind, and she accuses her generation of being blind. Her generation was born to an ideological atmosphere but revolted against it. She expresses hope that the new generation will triumph where her generation failed to establish a new system based on "democracy, secularism, social justice, freedom, the mother tongue, and territorial and legal integrity."[13]

In both its bold assessments and its glaring failures, Hedayat's letter is a historical document written by a dedicated and principled revolutionary activist who, at barely forty-two years old, has served multiple jail sentences because of her political convictions. With remarkable tenacity it speaks truth to power and shares her visions of a liberated and democratic future. It is certainly not a document to be compared to, say, Gramsci's *Prison Notebooks*. It lacks depth of philosophical erudition and political imagination. But it is a document to be compared to Martin Luther King Jr.'s August 1963 "Letter from Birmingham Jail." Perhaps the most sig-

nificant aspect of the letter is the way it declares the death of the
Reform Movement of which she and other political activists like
her had pushed forward. She blames herself and denounces those
who had systematically compromised the more daring dimensions
of the reformist aspirations. She passes the baton to the next generation, a generation that she now tasks with altogether dismantling
the corrupt ruling regime.

The limitations of the letter are rooted in Hedayat's lack of geopo-
litical perception, the enduring calamity of the totalitarian pedagogy
in an Islamic republic, the almost universal appeal of neoliberalism,
in the lack of resources, in the haphazard learning of a generation
that relies primarily on social media and the internet, but above all in
the just and understandable anger against the Islamic Republic. All
these factors and more come together to tilt her political judgment.
Evident in the entire texture of the prose is a cliché-ridden assumption about what, without the slightest hesitation, she calls "the West"
and "Western pseudo intellectuals"—entirely oblivious of vast
demographic changes that have radically altered the moral, political,
and critical apparatus of life in Europe and the United States. With
phrases such as "Western intellectual circles" and "Western intellectuals," she gives away the fact that she is unaware of what has happened in the UK or the United States or France or Australia or New
Zealand, where Arab, Muslim, African, Caribbean, Latin American, Southeast Asian, and, yes, even Iranian thinkers have recast
the very intellectual landscape. In her mind, alas, she still thinks of
Western intellectuals as blue-eyed, blonde-haired German or French
philosophers, and what a trajectory of thinkers like Edward Said or
Gayatri Spivak or Tariq Ali or Homi Bhabha or Pankaj Mishra or V.
Y. Mudimbe or Enrique Dussel or Walter Mignolo has done over the
last half century eludes her critical imagination.

The evidence of this regrettable limitation in a leading revolutionary activist is in Hedayat's assessment of Islamophobia,
which is quite crucial and needs careful attention, for she is right
that something serious is happening in the commencement of the
Zhina uprising with the burning of scarves, but she is not quite
clear as to what, exactly, the burning of scarves means. She is
rightly concerned she might be accused of Islamophobia, for if
she does not understand the meaning of that symbolic act, and
she evidently does not, then she is indeed Islamophobic, in the
same rank as the platoon of Islamophobic monarchists flooding
the internet, and hopefully she might be horrified to find herself
in their company. "I shit on Islam," read a placard in Berlin during
a massive Iranian protest on behalf of the Zhina uprising, and
under it repeated, "and I shit on the other Islam which you say is
different." Right there, under that sign, is where Hedayat would
find herself if she does not carefully think through what she says.
If she does not understand the battle against mandatory hijab, she
will also find herself in the company of rank charlatans like Ayaan
Hirsi Ali or Masih Alinejad and the entire Islamophobic industry they represent. What these protesters are saying and doing
is not against hijab per se but against mandatory hijab, therefore
against the patriarchal violence of forced veiling and for the freedom of choice—to wear or not to wear the hijab. Hateful, and
justly so, of the ruling Islamist regime, writing literally from jail,
Hedayat is rightly angry with the Islamist regime, but that hatred,
alongside an ignorance of the battlefield of xenophobia in what
she calls "the West," which includes but is not limited to Islamophobia, blinds her to what is happening under her own nose: a
far superior movement for choice that is not in opposition but in
fact in tandem with what is happening in those progressive circles

she sarcastically dismisses and puts in scare quotes. Hedayat is a courageous revolutionary activist but astonishingly limited in her critical awareness, and because of this, she unwitting aligns with reactionary monsters.

MANDATORY VEILING, MANDATORY UNVEILING: POLICING WOMEN'S BODIES

Perhaps the most startling aspect of Bahareh Hedayat's position on mandatory hijab is her historical amnesia. Only one dynasty earlier, her mother's generation was subjected to the vile and brutish mandatory unveiling of Reza Shah, designed to make Iran look more like the Europe of his dictatorial imagination. The terror that the ruling Islamist ideologues, the Salafi and Taliban-like component of the ruling regime in Iran, perpetrate on its citizens is not limited to but starts with regulating the dress codes of Iranian women, particularly the poor and middle-class Iranian women. Women in the richer and more opulent parts of Tehran care little for such codes and for the so-called morality police, which is itself formed mostly of poor and middle-class families. The power dynamic here between the rich and the poor and the powerful and the powerless reveals a systemic banality that defines the very fabric of Iranian society under the rule of the Islamic regime. In the not-so-distant historical past and in the immediate richer parts of the city and the country, the whole issue of mandatory veiling is put in radically different contexts.

Decades of US sanctions against Iran have exacerbated the frightful chasm between the very poor and the obscenely rich in Iran. The supporters and enablers of the ruling regime have amassed astronomical wealth through shady business practices and deep-rooted corruption. In a 2009 essay, Djavad Salehi-Isfahani, a widely respected US-based Iranian economist, summed up the postrevolutionary condition succinctly:

> Inside Iran the facts regarding the evolution of equality are hotly debated. However, data from the Statistical Center of Iran offer evidence of how inequality has changed in terms of household expenditures, education attainment, and access to health and basic services. The picture that emerges is a mixed one: success in improving the standard of living and the quality of life for the poor, and failure in improving the overall distribution of income.[14]

There is no understanding of the Zhina uprising and the issue of mandatory veiling outside the economic factors that have afflicted the Islamist theocracy for decades.

Since the publication of this essay in 2009, things have drastically changed for the worse—at least in part because of US sanctions. While the social uprising during 2017 and 2018, just a decade after the publication of that article, was mostly fueled by the poor and for economic reasons, the current uprising has linked those enduring economic problems with the more middle-class social concerns over mandatory veiling and the abusive behavior of the state toward women. As the 2017–2018 uprising revealed the economic fault lines of the ruling regime, the protests triggered by the death of Mahsa Zhina Amini while in police custody reveal the frustrated aspirations of a highly able and wired generation with a different conception of themselves than the totalitarian state allows them to express. There is no separating the economic and social dimensions of any political uprising.

Despite the coalescence of other equally if not more important economic issues, at the heart of these current protests is the
veiling of Iranian women against their will. To be sure, millions of
Iranian women wear the hijab voluntarily and proudly as a sign of
their faith and identity. But millions of other women do not wish
for the practice to be violently imposed on them. The mandatory
veiling that was initiated soon after the Islamic Republic took over
was a direct challenge to the mandatory unveiling that Reza Shah
Pahlavi had imposed on Iranian women when he took power in the
1930s. Two tyrants, Reza Shah and Ayatollah Khomeini, focused
on policing women's bodies as the site of their respective ideologies of power and domination, one giving a "modern" garb and the
other an "Islamic" garb to their respective tyrannies. The first massive social protest against the Islamic Republic's mandatory veiling
took place on International Women's Day, March 8, 1979. More
than forty years later, the Islamic Republic has miserably failed
to impose its policing of women's bodies on its defiant citizens.
The issue at hand, as a result, is not veiling. It is mandatory veiling. Even voluntary veiling would compromise and diminish the
tyrannical terror of the ruling regime. Wearing the veil voluntarily
is as disruptive of that tyranny as not wearing it.

What we are witnessing in Iran in the imposition of mandatory veiling is the reverse of what we see in much of Europe and
North America, where Muslim women are systematically harassed
if they choose to wear the hijab. For decades, not a single day has
passed without a racist, misogynist, bigoted violent attack on Muslim women in Europe and the United States. According to the
Southern Poverty Law Center, the highly respected institution
that documents hate crimes, "Anti-Muslim hate groups . . . largely
appeared after the Sept. 11, 2001, terrorist attacks and mix racism

and anti-immigrant ideas. Their rise breeds a climate of fear, hate and intimidation directed toward Muslims or those perceived to be Muslim."[15] Muslim women who wear the hijab are the primary target of this whole industry of Islamophobia, for they are the most visible. These crimes are not just the work of a gang of racist goons funded by Islamophobic millionaires. Throughout Europe as well as the United States legislation has targeted Muslim women and the hijab. Full or partial bans of the hijab have been introduced in Austria, France, Belgium, Denmark, Bulgaria, the Netherlands, Germany, Italy, Spain (in some localities of Catalonia), Switzerland, Norway, and elsewhere. What the Islamist theocracy is doing in Iran is the exact reverse of what Reza Shah did just a generation earlier, or what the ruling Islamophobic regimes do in Europe and the United States, as the bodies of women are the identical site of this injustice on both sides of the divide.

In a major article for *Hastings Race and Poverty Law Journal* in 2018, Aliah Abdo writes: "The First Amendment of the United States Constitution guarantees freedom of religion, however the current sociopolitical and legal climate has allowed for various restrictions on hijab, the headscarf worn by Muslim women."[16] The article, titled "The Legal Status of Hijab in the United States," details "restrictions and bans affecting the wearing of hijab in educational settings, employment, prison entry, state driver license photos, athletic competitions, airports, and in court, noting an alarming trend both internationally and domestically." These are also women, also human beings, also entitled to their rights to choose what an entire generation of political activists like Bahareh Hedayat fails to see—not just that women must be free to wear the hijab as much as opt not to wear it, but failure to understand what the Zhina uprising is about: freedom of choice, not the freedom to deny that power to any woman who wishes to wear the hijab.

Forced unveiling in the United States or Europe is as pernicious as forced veiling in Iran, Afghanistan, or any other part of the Muslim-majority countries. Both practices, though opposite of each other in appearance, are identical in reality, turning the body of a Muslim woman into a battleground of opposing ideologies of bodily control and biopower. Insisting on the choice and the right to wear the hijab is therefore as vital in the United States and Europe as the right not to wear it in places like Iran or Afghanistan. The world at large and the subjugation of women can no longer allow for hypocrisy and double standards. No European country or the United States can denounce the abusive behavior of the Iranian state while harboring the most vicious forms of Islamophobia targeting Muslim women in their own countries.

The violent behavior of the ruling Islamist regime in Iran is a cause of concern and embarrassment for those Muslim women in or out of Iran who choose to wear hijab, and for them it is a matter of pride and identity. Hedayat may go back to jail because of her battles against an Islamist tyranny, but still she is not in a position to deny that right to any other woman who refuses to join in unveiling out of her own equally compelling wishes and rights. It is impossible to imagine a Muslim woman who chooses to wear the hijab in the United States or Europe or anywhere else to condone its violent imposition on women who do not wish to wear it. The death of Mahsa Zhina Amini in Iran has already marked a massive social uprising across the country, once again revealing for the whole world that the ruling Islamic regime has violently imposed a draconian jurisprudence of fear and intimidation to sustain its tyrannical hold on power. The propaganda, security, intelligence, and military apparatus of the Islamic Republic may or may not succeed in crushing this uprising like it has all its previous gestations. But the indubitable fact remains that the Islamic Republic as a state apparatus has categorically failed to generate an iota of legitimacy for itself more than forty years after it stole the dreams and aspirations of a democratic future for millions of Iranians.

Toward that democratic future, the most significant positive outcome that can happen from this uprising is if globally conscious and aware women were to lead it and define its course and consequences. But "women" should not be taken as a generic term—two intersections are crucial: the dynamics of class and the symbolism of veiling. The legitimate cause of women's choice in wearing or not wearing the hijab must intersect with the dynamics between the working- and the middle-class prerogatives. When veiled and unveiled women, working- and middle-class women, come together to lead this uprising then we have an uprising to behold. No one speaks for Mahsa Zhina Amini except the loud but muted voices of a massive social uprising in search of the terms of its own emancipation. We all need to put our ears to the ground and listen carefully. The subaltern around the world do not speak English.[17]

HOW IRANIAN CINEMA ANTICIPATED THE ZHINA UPRISING

The limitations of Bahareh Hedayat in understanding the Zhina uprising are overcompensated by something hiding in plain sight. As always, the most potent evidence of a social uprising is on public display for the whole world to see in visual and performing arts. No social uprising of the magnitude we were witnessing in Iran since mid-September 2022, and led principally by women of all social classes and economic backgrounds from across the country and specifically for women's rights, is entirely beyond and above its historical and cultural contexts. At the same time, such historic movements should not be reduced and assimilated backward to what we already know about the history and culture of these societies. We therefore have a dual balancing task at hand, of both marking the historical and cultural roots of this movement and yet allowing its unfolding to teach us something very specific about its nature and disposition.

Assimilating this uprising backward to what we already know about these societies is a logical and analytical fallacy. The world changes, societies grow into and out of their histories, the tyranny of the past is the first to be dismantled in such youthful movements. Iran in the fall of 2022, just as Egypt in the winter of 2011, was on the edge of a new era. These uprisings may or may not result in any tangible political results. But the societies that have given birth to them will never be the same as they were before the frenzy of these uprisings. In this regard the sustained course of Iranian film, fiction, drama, music, and poetry of the last half century has had a crucial role to play—for, by nature, such cultural artifacts are polyfocal and multisignificatory and they don't mean just one thing. They occasion a certain understanding of their society, but at the same time, given the allegorical disposition of their visual and performing artistry, they also point to something beyond their evident realities. It is not accidental that a leading filmmaker like Jafar Panahi and a host of his colleagues were summarily arrested and jailed by the ruling Islamist tyranny soon after the commencement of the Zhina uprising, afraid not of what they may say, but of what their cinema has already entailed.[18]

A good example of such cultural artifacts is the case of Iranian cinema of the last half century, to be safe and pragmatic and not to expand the domain to any larger, though still significant, frame of reference. At the outset we must understand that the very architecture of visual and performing arts in Iran, as elsewhere, has radically altered and been digitized. This generation reads more Facebook than books, watches more video clips on Instagram and YouTube than full movies in theaters. The digital age has radically shortened their attention span, as the logic of the tweeter has seriously shortened their patience for complicated sentences with more than one subordinate clause. But still, in the very subconscious shores of their thoughts, images, and passages of their long and winding past shimmer with power and tenacity.

The issue to be noted is the youthful character of the Zhina uprising, which corresponds to the youthful character of Iranian cinema and the centrality of children and young adults in the entire legacy of leading filmmakers like Abbas Kiarostami, Amir Naderi, Bahram Beizai, Jafar Panahi, and many other major and minor figures. The children of this cinematic legacy are precocious, prematurely and overtly political, made so by not just their parental generation that was harboring revolutionary romances but by children's authors, filmmakers, poets, and artists who had invested so much in their artwork for the future generation. This is that future generation.

Take, for example, Amir Naderi's *Harmonica* (1974), where we encounter a boy who chances upon a harmonica with which he tyrannizes his friends, demanding and exacting obedience from them to allow them to play his magic instrument. The boy sports a haircut with an uncanny resemblance to a crown or a turban. Since its release in 1974, *Harmonica* has traversed back and forth into the deepest thickets of Iranian history, explaining how, when the late Shah chanced upon a bonanza of oil revenue (harmonica) in the aftermath of the Arab oil embargo of 1973, he tyrannized his people—just as any other crowned or turbaned tyrant in distant or recent history of the nation has done. My generation did not just become politicized with these films. We learned how to live our lives despite the tyranny they marked.

The more important issue of the Zhina uprising is the material and iconic vigilance of women of all walks of life in this uprising, which points to the exceptional power and presence of Iranian women as producers, directors, actors, editors, sound designers, members of the production team, the cast, the crew, and above all the subject of Iranian cinema. The world should not be fooled by the white-passing young women the US-EU media glitz in this uprising. The word "women" in its slogan refers to the embattled, bitter, massively impoverished, unemployed, underemployed, and battered working-class women from Kurdistan to Baluchistan, to the darkest corners of that brutalized country, whom you never see on the cover of any magazine. Yes, the monarchists, the born-again Pahlavi diehards, and the upper-middle-class expats sporting their Lamborghinis in Los Angeles with the phrase "Women, Life, Freedom" plastered on them have as much a right to be part of this movement as anyone else. But their vision of what needs to be done and the vision of the structurally impoverished and doubly brutalized working-class women who never see the light of a camera are vastly different.

What about those real women? The cinema of Bahram Beizai stands as the hallmark of a sustained body of work in which he has paid exceptional attention to Iranian women.[19] Exactly in the opposite direction of Beizai is Masoud Kimiai, who has dwelled on patriarchal archetypes of Iranian women. In the middle of the two iconic filmmakers stands the remarkable oeuvre of Dariush Mehrjui and his famous trilogy—*Sara* (1993), *Pari* (1995), and *Leila* (1996)—where he has given Iranian cinema a detailed encounter with the trials and tribulations of middle-class women. In this regard the presence of some leading female filmmakers, such as Rakhshan Bani-Etemad, Pouran Derakhshandeh, Tahmineh Milani, Marzieh Boroumand, Manijeh Hekmat, Marzieh Meshkini, Samira Makhmalbaf, and scores of others, has brought the specific issues of women to even sharper focus. Marzieh Meshkini's *The Day I Became a Woman* (2000) is a singularly iconic film to watch at this moment; in three successive episodes she portrays the debilitating fate of women in a repressive Islamist regime.[20] All these films and many others like them have been extremely prescient about what is happening today—but still the drama, the stories, the heroic deeds, the tragic ends, and the symbolic echoes of this uprising remain to be fully canvassed and understood. Names such as Mahsa Zhina Amini, Abolfazl Adinehzadeh, Sarina Esmailzadeh, Kumar Daroftadeh, Asra Panahi, Kian Pirfalak, Nika Shakarami, Hadis Najafi, and those of so many other young women and men viciously murdered by the security forces of the Islamic Republic have gut-wrenching stories yet to be told.

The particular combination of the three words "Zan, Zendegi, Azadi" is crucial here. In one slogan the whole project of "intersectionality," as theorized and widely explored by my Columbia colleague Kimberlé Crenshaw, is fully evident. For while sustaining the centrality of the doubly tyrannized reality of Iranian women, it adds the economic factor of living in dignity and the political project of freedom to achieve it.[21] The devil is, of course, in the details. Consider another iconic Iranian film, the undisputed masterpiece of Kurdish Iranian filmmaker Bahman Ghobadi, *A Time for Drunken Horses* (2000). It is a jewel of a film that he could never match in his illustrious but winding career. Depicting the brutalized lives of poor "smugglers" risking their lives and dignities to survive, the Kurdish origin of the slogan "Zan, Zendegi, Azadi" becomes evident when the young girl of the family is effectively sold as a child bride in exchange for a mule, as her older brother tries to take his handicapped younger brother to Iraqi Kurdistan for a lifesaving operation.[22]

In the three consecutive films of Jafar Panahi—*The Circle* (2000), *Crimson Gold* (2003), and *Offside* (2006)—we see the cycle of poverty-driven sex workers, the impoverished war veterans, and the prohibition of women attending sports events, all collected in one detailed account of what deeply ails Iranian society under the tyranny of the Islamic Republic. After watching these films one after the other, one can no longer wonder where the political and economic depth of this hatred toward the ruling regime emanates. These, do I need to add, are Iranian films, not Israeli, Saudi, or American films, or films bought and paid for by regime changers from abroad. The world ignores the solid evidence of what these deeply rooted cultural artifacts mean at the heavy cost of decency and integrity.

All these films and this entire cinematic legacy are crucial in helping us locate the current uprising in the right provenance. But still, the movement itself, like similar uprisings around the region and the world, have things to teach us beyond their history. There is, of course, nothing unusual or specific about women being integral to a social uprising. Women have had a powerful presence in all Iranian, Arab, and Muslim revolutions. Nobel laureates such as Yemeni activist Tawakkol Karman and Shirin Ebadi from Iran became emblematic of the rich and powerful presence of Muslim women in the destiny of their homelands. The powerful presence of Egyptian women in their revolution has revived the memory of the earlier generations of Inji Aflatoun, Latifa al-Zayyat, Doria Shafik, and Nawal al-Saadawi. Like their Arab counterparts, young Iranian women leading their uprising may not know who Huda Sha'arawi (1879–1947) was. But their uprising is not too dissimilar from that iconic moment when she defied public norms and unveiled herself. Generations later, Arab women may or may not opt to wear the hijab, but the defiant soul of Sha'arawi resonates in the power and dignity of their choices. What Iranian women are doing is not any different from what their sisters, mothers, and grandmothers have been doing across the Iranian, Arab, and Muslim world, in Egypt, Syria, Iraq, Tunisia, Morocco, and Palestine. Each of one of these uprisings has had its specific character, which takes serious scholarship and critical thinking to decipher. In that crucial task, just begun, particular attention has to be paid to how we recollect and reread the iconic artifacts of the past for the unfolding drama of the present.[23]

To understand the Zhina uprising is to come to terms with the fact that the outcome of this crucial event may continue to be in terms specific to Iranian moral imagination and cultural productions rather than in a sudden and abrupt collapse of the ruling regime—unless that collapse is the commencement of something even worse than the Islamic Republic itself. The fate of Iran as a country and a society is not separate from the political topography of the region and the world in which it is placed. The very act and fact of phantom liberties has always been stronger than the prospects of achieving it. But such phantom liberties are far more enabling and liberating than the illusion of democracy that a settler colony like Israel or a dysfunctional empire like the United States could even fathom. Ever since the Zhina uprising in Iran it has been a much happier social occasion to think of Iran and its defiant politics of revolt than of Israel and its murderous practices against Palestinians, or the United States and the prospect of a Donald Trump coming back to rule it.

TWO

THE NEXT IRANIAN REVOLUTION WILL NOT BE THEORIZED

Let us disregard potential consciousness or consciousness in the realm of ideas and talk about pragmatic consciousness, meaning a kind of consciousness that becomes evident in the course of people's struggles. All these forms of struggle are variations of the material and actualized consciousness that have come to the fore in the course of the Zhina uprising: armed guerrilla attack in the village of Persila; occupation of governors and mayors' offices and the hideout of their native informers; the daily protests of students on university campuses; crowds of people joining street protests; labor shut-downs and sit-downs by workers, truck drivers, and shopkeepers; participating in the mourning ceremonies on gravesites and turning them into sites of resistance and renewed battles—all to disregard all the instruments of repression and domination.

—**Shirin Kamangar** (March 2023)

Whether the ruling Islamist regime stays in power or falls, the Zhina uprising is always and already a revolutionary promise, not a delivery—the evidence of a democratic intuition in the making rather than a battle for a better constitution or a fairer election or a more handsome president—or even a younger Pahlavi monarch!

I have put forward the proposition that "democracy" is and always has been a delusion—and we are better off without it. I believe we Iranians have not learned the lessons of the coup of 1953—we did try democracy but the Americans and the British plotted a coup and aborted it—not just with bold-faced vulgarity but with conviction that democracy was not meant for us colored folks. We should learn our lessons. In the United States, we see racist gerrymandering ensuring that poor and powerless cannot hope for representative democracy. Revolutions in both their classical and contemporary gestations have also become as vacuous and untenable as the democracy they promise. We are better off ceasing to think in surgical terms of removing one tyranny and replacing it with another—for removing one is easy, replacing it with a better one an impossibility. The revolutionary conditions might threaten the status quo and the ruling states, but they will never dismantle them except to be replaced, via either a military coup or a foreign military intervention, or even worse a fascistic impulse toward totalitarianism, with a state even more tyrannical than the one they have overthrown. This is the simple fact, truth, and historical evidence of the Islamist regime succeeding the Pahlavi monarchy.

We are approaching the second quarter of the twenty-first century. There is absolutely no model of democracy anywhere in the world, including and particularly in the so-called West, to act as a blueprint for anywhere else in the world. As the oldest claim on democracy, the United States has been the singular cause of war, conquest, mayhem, mass deception, and misery around the globe, built on the sustained course of genocide of Native Americans and the transatlantic slave trade. Those are not things of the past. They are definitive to the present circumstances of the United States, with indelible marks of white supremacy in its political culture. Donald Trump is America and America is Donald Trump. As the events of January 6, 2021, showed clearly, for the whole world to see, the instant their chosen messiah is not acknowledged by the democratic majority, Trump's supporters would rather burn those pantheons of law and order to the ground. The gentlest, most respectable polities like those in Sweden or Norway or Finland or Denmark have had their long socialist traditions devoured by globalized neoliberalism, the rise of neo-Nazi outfits, and the encroaching power of NATO military alliances underlined by a military industry that provides much of the hardware to maim and murder people in darker continents. The Russian invasion of Ukraine has failed to carve out a part of Europe into Eurasia, but it has succeeded spectacularly in militarizing the entirety of Europe and its NATO alliance. Popular uprisings like the one in Iran are therefore historic moments to think through the prospects of the post-democratic world where we all live.

The Zhina uprising of 2022 to 2023 set the Iranian scene and ushered it onto the global stage; it demands and will have to exact an explanation, not just of itself but of the world. Both in its promises and particularly in its fascistic underbelly, it is about to show the world a path beyond their limited imagination. Though we may not be entirely convincing in our demands and expectations, theories and meditations, the world can scarce ignore us. So, what is the solution at this historic juncture? A democratic state is a delusion. Voluntary associations, I have proposed, standing in between the ruling states and the atomized individuals are the only way a measure of self-governance might be procured. Independent labor unions, grassroots women's rights organizations, and nationwide student assemblies: these are what I propose to be the solution. If you were to read Shirin Kamangar's participant observations in her "Naqd-e Birahmaneh Khizesh Tudeh-i Ari, Amma Cheguneh?" (Brutal Criticism of the Mass Uprising Yes, But How?), this is what you would notice: a constellation of militant or moderate activism ranging from guerrilla attacks on police stations to industrial actions by truck drivers to mourning ceremonies turned political on gravesites—these are where the real political events happen.[1] Beyond such traumatic moments we need to think of more enduring forms of voluntary associations and collective actions.

But what stands in the way of this full realization?

"RAW FURY"

"In Iran, Raw Fury Is in the Air" read the title of a fine piece by Robert F. Worth quite early in the uprising in mid-September 2022. Having covered the 2009 protests, dubbed "the Green Movement," Mr. Worth reported that these uprisings had a different tone:

> This time, raw fury is in the air, a sense that protesters are girding themselves for war rather than liberation. Their chants suggest a new spirit of intransigence: "We will fight, we will die, we will get Iran back." The protesters don't seem to have illusions about their country blooming into democracy; this is not an Iranian spring. They are not inclined toward politics as a vehicle for change, and that in

itself is a troubling sign. If the protests have one theme, it seems to be sheer hatred of the Iranian regime.[2]

That raw fury and that sheer hatred have a history and an unforeseen course of unfolding. Mr. Worth is correct that protesters have had no expectations to see their country bloom into a democracy, or that the Iranian version of the Arab Spring is about to happen (look what the Arab Spring did for the Arabs!). But that is not "a troubling sign." To the contrary: that is the greatest feature of this unfolding cycle of uprisings. The guiding principle I propose in this reading of the Zhina uprising is to see this raw fury as the sign of the end of the postcolonial state, not a moment too soon, and with it the end of postcolonialism that I proposed at the commencement of the Arab revolutions of 2010 to 2011.[3] I had worked my way to this conclusion at least since my book, *Iran without Borders: Towards A Critique of the Postcolonial Nation* (2016), which was the birth of the idea of the stateless nation in my thinking.

The next Iranian revolution will therefore not be televised, namely staged for success or failure, as Gil Scott-Heron's 1970 iconic poem would have it: "The Revolution Will Not Be Televised."

I celebrate this prospect rather than mourn it for very specific reasons. Following what Asef Bayat has aptly identified as a phase of *Post-Islamism* (2013), expanding into his argument regarding *Life as Politics* (2013) leading to *Revolution without Revolutionaries* (2017), I have pushed forward in articulating the terms of the *Inevitable Demise of the Nation-State* (2020)—where we need to come to terms with the idea of revolution in a radically different way. The next Iranian revolution will not be staged for a television or Instagram livestreaming—for it is already happening somewhere else. Only through the combined force of voluntary associations of labor unions, women's rights organizations, and student assemblies, or another similar kind of substate formation would the state's monopoly of violence be confronted. States have assumed a life of their own, with minimal to nonexistent connections to the totality of the people they falsely claim to represent. This is true of all states, not just the Islamic Republic. If we are still to believe in the veracity of any revolution, we need to seek its location off the glaring cameras, as it were, focused as they are on the failings of the ruling states.

The "sheer hatred" of which Mr. Worth writes marks the moment when Iran was once again engulfed in massive protests in almost all its major cities. But the ending of those uprisings would not be like the time when the late Shah boarded a plane and left Iran, or when Hosni Mubarak left his presidential palace, or any other such dramatic scene set for television. Yes, masses of protesters have poured into the streets, women have burned their scarves, scores of demonstrators were killed, thousands arrested, a few publicly hanged, while the internet was slowed down to calm and control the web to prevent further unrest. The cause of the uprising was and remains just and legitimate—the tyrannical rule of an incompetent clerical class and their praetorian militia, the Revolutionary Guards, deep corruption of state officials, massive inflation, and scores of other economic and social malice. Against the waves of protests, the regime's deadly spikes were out, as were the separatist ethnic nationalists demanding autonomy from the central state, while the expat protests remained useless or worse. Israel, Saudi Arabia, and the United States sought to benefit from the turmoil—not to dismantle the ruling regime in Iran but to weaken it even more at the negotiating table of the nuclear deal. All of that was at work, but this regime will not fall, and if it does, it will be either by a military coup of its own organs or else by a foreign intervention—neither of which turns the script in any democratic direction.

What was paramount, meanwhile, was the effective partition of the nation from the state that had laid a false claim on its legitimacy—that was and remains the only palpable victory. This publicly staged partition is permanent, for the ruling emperor (ayatollah) is naked, and the myth of the postcolonial state is exposed for the lie that it has always been. Wael Hallaq is right in his *Impossible State* (2012) that any state claim to Islam is an impossibility, as is Asef Bayat about the stage of post-Islamism, and thus my conclusion one step further toward the dismantling of the delusion of the postcolonial nation-state. The next revolution will therefore not be theorized either, as the previous ones, or televised, tweeted, or posted on social media. The demented scale of social media, meant and designed for the tweets of Donald Trump and Elon Musk, have no patience or capacity for that quiet, subterranean revolution. The next revolution has already happened in the active partition of the nations and the states that do not represent them anymore—if they ever did. Toppling those states is no longer the objective of these uprisings, for the postcolonial state is now completely exposed as a lie, while the neoliberal dream of the regime changers is too little too late. "Raw fury," indeed! For good reasons, and even better purposes.

THE LIE OF THE NATION-STATE

What would be the shape of such an undying revolt—a final dismantling of the lie of the nation-state much of the world has inherited from its brutal encounter with European colonial modernity, when a gun was put to their heads and they were told they were now free, secular, and modern to think? Alternatives are elsewhere—with the wretched of the earth. Look at Black Lives Matter, or look at the

struggles of Palestinians: just as the United States will not fall under
the weight of BLM, neither will the Israeli garrison state pack up and
go to Washington, DC, because Palestinians resist their homeland
being stolen from under their feet. But people go on living (or else
they die) richer, nobler, and more enabling lives, freed from the delusion of tyrants and charlatans and the democracies they promise. The
Islamist regime ruling Iran and its brutality is its own undoing, as
it keeps blaming everyone except itself. Under its garrison state the
Islamist regime (just like its Zionist counterpart) has systematically
destroyed any semblance of group affiliation that could have resisted
its fascism. Meanwhile, the Saudi-Israeli-US alliance is not responsible for this unrest, but they will be its beneficiaries. In the Zhina
uprising, the leadership of Iranian women is not a mere formalism—
it is real. Veiling or unveiling is symptomatic of something else: it is
the freedom to choose, following generations of sustained struggles
that have ultimately come to this. The result ahead harkens to the
third-world feminism of figures as radical as Chandra Mohanty or as
liberal as Lila Abu-Lughod. Poor and disenfranchised women worldwide, those in Iran included, are the subaltern of the subaltern—
they question not just this state but all states, not just this dictator
but all dictators. Yet the banality of ethnic nationalism of one brand
or another would have us convinced that all women would mirac-
ulously overcome endemic patriarchy under different states or that
they should prefer a Kurdish misogynist tyrant over a "Persian"!

We can therefore look at this uprising as the final crescendo of
the 1977 to 1979 revolution itself, which had the seeds of its own
undoing, though here there is a "death to" but no corresponding
"long live" to match it. Like all other uprisings, this one is also
against tyranny, but it is not for anything else. As I said when I was
writing on the Arab Spring, here, too, we need to change the *regime*

de savoir, for we have moved away from total to open-ended revolutions, to a revolution that can no longer be theorized for it is not geared toward any formal state. The prose and poetry of the narrative have moved from epic to novel to tragedy to a postmodern revolution lacking any metanarrative, where the very episteme of reading social uprisings is being redefined. The Zhina uprising is the final demise of the project of colonial modernity—a postcolonial termination of colonial modernity—with which both the extended shadows of European colonialism and the "modernity" it had occasioned have been epistemically exhausted. The ruling states have been totally absorbed into the geopolitics of the region, and the nations they falsely claimed for themselves have disappeared into vulnerable multitudes, and the country they share degenerated into a garrison state for the operation of the state, like Israel—a state without a nation ruling over a nation without a state. We have all been turned into stateless Palestinians, as all our ruling states have become like Israel, murderous regimes ruling over atomized natives.

What we are witnessing in Iran is a massive social staging of a post-democratic uprising, where the globally rehearsed rhetoric of liberal democracy has lost all legitimacy and is a shallow ideological positioning without substance, bolstered by mass media deception, rather than a classic case of ideological positioning, party politics, and revolutionary momentum. The ruling Islamist regime is a garrison state and works like an occupation force engaged with other garrison states for the mutual preservation of the ruling states. The democratic aspirations of nations are potent but vacuous so far as its advocates are expat careerists who look more like their local celebrities than like leaders of a national uprising millions of miles away. What is therefore happening is not the classical case of any revolutionary momentum that will lead to toppling the regime, for even if that were to happen, the façade of the legitimate state will still crumble and its military will show its angry face. In light of that vested and invested force of the state, the post-democratic uprisings will work only through small-scale voluntary and professional associations like women's rights organizations, student assemblies, and labor unions—where the state remains as potent or weak as its regional geopolitics allow it but systematically challenged by internal substate forces. Social forces are forming along multiple axes but not in direct confrontation with the garrison state, which remains purely interested in self-preservation. The dynamics of that form of social revolution are endemic, slow in mobilization, nondramatic in delivery, and entirely outside the parameters of the attention span of social media. To remain a promise and stay shy of any false delivery, this uprising maps a different kind of liberation, not from the tyranny of state, but from the moral, imaginative, and material compliance with that tyranny. Civil disobedience here has assumed an entirely revolutionary disposition but not a revolutionary end toward a final state. The lie of the postcolonial state is finally exposed.

Against these odds, though, the nostalgia for a final and total state persists apace and galore.

A POSTHUMOUS INDICTMENT

Soon after Kiumars Pourahmad's suicide at the age of seventy-three on April 5, 2023, in northern Iran, the news came out that a novel published a couple of years earlier outside Iran, *Ma Hameh Sharik-e Jorm Hastim* (*We Are All Accomplices*, 2021) under the pseudonym Hamid Hamed was actually penned by him. People began to read the novel with a renewed interest. The London-based publisher announced a free PDF copy of the book would be made available for Iranians living inside Iran. BBC Persian reported that some 260,000 people had downloaded the book soon after this news, whereas a regular print in Iran would run about a couple of hundred or so.[4]

Who was Kiumars Pourahmad and what was the novel about? And why does that matter?

Kiumars Pourahmad (1949–2023) was a major Iranian film-maker, not globally known or celebrated like other luminaries of the field, but students of Iranian cinema knew him well and admired some of his major works like *Beh Khater-e Hanieh* (For the Sake of Hanieh) (1995). Pourahmad had also worked with the late Abbas Kiarostami and had written a book detailing his reflections on Kiarostami's cinema. Three different facts had come together to make his sudden passing a traumatic event. First the fact that at the mature age of seventy-three he had decided to take his own life; second that he had spent a lifetime being a respected member of the Iranian film community; and then the surprising news that he had actually written a novel and published it anonymously for fear of censorship and persecution abroad.

The novel *We Are all Accomplices* tells the story of Arash. Born to wealth, power, and prestige, the young protagonist opts to go to a small village to educate young children. The story takes place in the 1960s at the height of the Pahlavi power. Arash has a palpably positive impact on the village, especially for women who now achieve their rightful place. From this premise rises an unabashed celebration of the Pahlavi regime and a solid denunciation of religious fanaticism and "superstition" that had ensued under the Islamic Republic. The Islamic revolution had put an end to that paradise and inaugurated a hell. There is much more than a ring of truth to the terror of censorship and hardship of all sorts under the Islamic Republic the novel depicts, but also much more than a cup of nostalgia for the Pahlavi regime, which flows from Pourahmad's pen as God's gift to humanity. Even in his films, Pourahmad was not exactly a subtle or meditative filmmaker, but still there was a patience about his work. But not here in this novel—where the disguise of a pseudonym gave him license to pour out all the tormented memories of a lifetime of trying to make films asunder an Islamic republic.

The novel became something of a last will and testament, in which Pourahmad shared his anger against an Islamist militancy that had mentally tortured him and his colleagues with mind-boggling censorship. The intolerable circumstances of life under the Islamist regime had pushed some major Iranian filmmakers like Bahram Beizai and Mohsen Makhmalbaf out of the country. Others like Abbas Kiarostami, Dariush Mehrjui, Jafar Panahi, and Mohammad Rasoulof had remained and learned to cope with the censorship. There was much in the novel with which the entire nation, and artists and filmmakers in particular, would identify. But there was more to the novel than just an account of the horrors of the ruling regime.

The novel as a novel is not much to note or celebrate. It is just a vehicle to share Pourahmad's political thoughts, which consist of the Pahlavis being a lovely regime and the Islamic Republic being a horrible hell—a portrait drawn with a thick and wide brush with very little reflection or effort to hide behind the characters. Though not entirely in the same bold and pronounced ways, a nostalgia for the Pahlavis was very much in the air soon after the start of the Zhina uprising. The monarchists were hoping and planning to ride the Zhina uprising and bring the last Pahlavi prince, tucked away for over forty years in the United States, back to ascend the peacock throne. Putting the widespread nostalgia to effective political use, the renewed Pahlavism was underwritten by an unabashed dose of fascism that had been launched online with a hatred of Islam, Muslims, Arabs, and the left as definitive to it. "Molla, chapi, mojahed," or "the mullah, the leftist, and the mojahed," had been turned into a curse by the monarchists, screaming it at anyone who disagreed or even appeared to opposed them.

ISLAMISM AS PARADOX

Nostalgia for Pahlavi monarchism and the ruling Islamist militancy had a common denominator: statism of the most potent sort, at a time when the very centrality of the nation-state itself was an outdated proposition. In an off-the-cuff remark (but isn't his entire "philosophy" an off-the-cuff remark?) about Iran, Slavoj Žižek proposes a paradox about the hypocrisy of "the Western left,"

> which to a large extent ignores the phenomenal liberal "renaissance" that is going on in Iran's civil society . . . the left makes no fuss when leading figures of this movement lose their jobs and are arrested etc. . . . However, one should nonetheless raise the more fundamental question: is bringing Western liberal democracy the true solution for getting rid of the religious fundamentalist regime, or are these regimes rather a symptom of liberal democracy itself? What to do in cases like that of Algeria or the Palestinian territories where a "free" democratic election brings "fundamentalists" to power?[5]

Even disregarding a cliché-ridden and flawed reading of the events in Iran, these vacuous ideological markers—from "Western left" to "liberal renaissance" to "religious fundamentalism" as opposed to "Western liberal democracies"—feel vacuous and meaningless when a grassroots social uprising is afoot. But at the root of all such ideological haggling between the left and the right, between liberal democracy that is supposed to be "Western" and Islamic fundamentalism that is supposed to be "non-Western," remains a constant reactionary *statism* that sees everything from the vantage point of the ruling regime, of one sort or another. That outdated position is the flawed discourse that needs to be once and for all dismantled.

Let us have a quick flashback to more than a decade before the commencement of the Zhina uprising, when this prevalent statism had a particularly potent force. When the Green Movement started in Iran in June 2009, there was a recalcitrant faction of the left that rampaged against it and denounced the civil rights uprising as a Saudi-US plot to dismantle the Islamic Republic, appease Israel, and pave the way for neoliberal imperialism. About two years after the Green Movement and a year into the Arab Spring, the selfsame segment of the left faced an even more crippling dilemma trying to formulate a sensible position vis-à-vis the bloody drama in Syria. As I said at the time:[6] to be fair and to understand the predicament of the left vis-à-vis the Arab Spring in general and the Syrian uprising in particular, we must first have a clear conception of the right to which the left was in part reacting. The position of the right was self-evident: the Syrian regime is a murderous tyranny, it is butchering its own citizens, and "the international community" (by which they mean the United States and its European and regional allies through their machinations at the UN, the Gulf Cooperation Council, and the Arab League) must intervene to prevent the bloodbath, and any one raising the slightest question about that narrative is an accomplice in the murderous acts of Bashar al-Assad.

To be sure, the self-serving chicanery of the right's position, which is either morally blind or intellectually challenged, was incapable of seeing the hypocrisy of the US/NATO position, cherry-picking their "humanitarian intervention" and thus encouraging the rush to the position that the left had assumed. But that tit for tat was and remains a useless tautology and would not help clarify the fault lines of the left beyond its habitual dilemmas. The problem with both these positions—the left and the right—is that they speak from a *statist* position, a sprint to grab hold of the state apparatus and replace it as it falls. The right spoke from behind the US-Israeli guns and from behind the Saudi bank accounts, and the left from a position of resisting that power and wishing to support an existing, evolving, or emerging state apparatus that could ensure that resistance. What the left and the right shared, however, was their identical *statism*, because, for them, those entire Arab revolutions were about taking control of the *state* apparatus, of *state* power, of steering the falling regimes of power to their own direction.

Categorically absent from the calculations of both the left and the right are the people, the real people, ordinary people, those who occupy the *public space*, people it, own it, fracture and fragment and fill it as labor unions, student assemblies, women's rights organizations, or any other kind of voluntary association. For the left and the right, knowingly or unknowingly, these people are mere puppets that are either used or abused for facilitating the US-Saudi machinations or else duped into revolutionary uprising that has been hijacked from them. Neither the left nor the right has the slightest trust, confidence, or even a politically potent conception of the *public space* that ordinary people physically and normatively occupy. The fundamental flaw of both the left and the right—one from intellectual limitation and the other out of moral deprivation—is that they have no ground-up conception of what it was that was unfolding in front of their eyes and was code-named "the Arab Spring." They are both *statists*—reaching to gain control of the *state* apparatus, or what Max Weber called "external means" of any state, its violent means of domination, forgetting what in the same sentence Weber called the necessity of "inner justification" on part of the people subject to those external means. Syrians, like all other Arabs from Morocco to Bahrain and down to Yemen, as indeed Iranians before and along with them in the rest of the Muslim world, have lost that "inner justification," and no "external means"—provided by the United States or Saudi Arabia or by Russia and the Islamic Republic—could force them into obedience.

They say you can conquer a land on horse, but you must descend in order to rule it—the same is true about Syria or any other part of the world. From the United States and Israel to Saudi Arabia and the Gulf states, and then from Russia and China to the Islamic Republic and Hezbollah, there certainly are many machinations at work to conquer Syria. But when all the dust is settled and these mighty machinations end, the new conquerors must come down to rule it—and when they do, they will find themselves facing the indomitable spirit of the people who have left their inner dungeons of fear—and who will never ever again be subject of either domestic tyranny or external treachery. The Arab Spring had unleashed the power of ordinary people and staged the *public space* they occupied and the civic associations they would eventually and inevitably form on that space. Again, as I said at the time, the Arab Spring had given birth to a robust revolutionary Gemeinschaft that will stay with these societies no matter who and what is in power. Unbeknownst to the political machinations that have divided the left and the right, the people of Syria—as indeed people from across the Arab and Muslim world—were dispelling their agoraphobia and realizing the power of their communal gatherings.

More than a decade later, the Zhina uprising spells out the same scenario. Islamism, just like its nemesis Zionism, has lost the historical game and totally exhausted itself. So has the liberal democracy that has given birth to Donald Trump, Ron DeSantis, and Tucker Carlson in the United States, a whole slew of proto-fascist politicians in Europe, and sustained the murderous BJP in power in India. The paradox that Slavoj Žižek thus identifies is no paradox at all, if he were to be delivered from the Eurocentric delusions of his own ideological positions. We, the entirety of humanity cured and liberated from the delusion of "the West" and its "liberal democracy" and all its colonial and postcolonial nemeses, are at the ground zero of facts of our fragile earth and exhausted ideologies, where only small voluntary associations can form the nuclei of moral and material resistance to state powers and sustain a measure of success and survival against all the reactionary ideologies, from "Islamic fundamentalism" to "western liberalism."

POSTCOLONIAL STATE AS A PARADOX GALORE

The collapse of the nation-state as a colonial project, the demise of the postcolonial state legitimacy with it, and the changing circumstances of revolutionary aspirations are also quite site-specific to the recent history of Iran itself. Offering a new perspective on Iran's politics and culture in the 1960s and 1970s, Ali Mirsepassi, in his book *Iran's Quiet Revolution: The Downfall of the Pahlavi State* (2019),

challenges the prevailing assumptions about prerevolutionary Iran.
He proposes that the political and cultural elites of the Pahlavi monarchy were partaking freely in what he identifies as "Gharbzadegi"
(Westoxication) discourses that would effectively contradict the
state's own "modernist" project. Projected as ideological alternatives to "Western-inspired" sentiments, these "antimodern" proclivities, Mirsepassi argues, influenced Iranian identity politics and
projected a "mystical" disposition. The Pahlavi regime was therefore
an "ideological gambler," inadvertently paving the path to its own
demise. Mirsepassi suggests that "a convergence of antimodern,
spiritual, and nativist discourse in both the Pahlavi state and the
Islamist revolutionary movement"[7] had paradoxically brought them
together. By focusing on the cultural transformations of the 1960s
and 1970s, Mirsepassi proposes that "the historical logic driving
the revolution along anti-secular and anti-Western paths becomes
considerably clarified."[8] His punchline is quite striking: "The com-
plicating factor in this picture is the Pahlavi state's pursuit of a Western and modernist model in economic and social policies, but an
ideologically anti-Western attitude in the cultural and even political
campaign to win public hegemony."[9]

In understanding Mirsepassi's argument, however, a few separate, quite incongruent, and disparate tracks will have to be carefully separated. The decidedly antimodern positions of a figure like
the mystic Heideggerian Ahmad Fardid (1910–1994), the position
of those critical of colonial modernity (but not antimodern) like
that of Jalal Al-e Ahmad, and the reactionary positivism of monarchists like Seyyed Hossein Nasr. These strands ought to be carefully
distinguished and separated from each other in order not to con-
flate them all as "nativist" antimodernity. The progressive aspects of
Iranian cinema, to which Mirsepassi pays closer attention, were not

critical of modernity or modernization, but critical of their fake and artificial disposition on the colonial end of European modernity. We therefore need to make a crucial distinction between antimodernity on mystical grounds (Fardid), a critique of modernity on colonial grounds (Al-e Ahmad), and positively reactionary "traditionalism" (Nasr) that was integral to Pahlavi state ideology.

Be that as it may, Mirsepassi makes a convincing argument regarding the integral contradictions of the ruling state ideology of the Pahlavi dynasty—wanting it both ways: to appear "modern" to foreigners and yet authentically mystical or "native" to Iranians. That tension had to do with the chimeric disposition of a postcolonial state, sharing an identical anxiety of legitimacy, pushing its roots in the Persepolis ruins, as it were, and yet speaking French with a Parisian accent to European heads of state. But this was more than a paradox—it was a definitive contradiction within the Pahlavi state that it could not resolve, not because it was gambling with its own future, but because it had embraced the central impossibility of the postcolonial state. The issue is the misconstrued category of mythology for a legitimate conception of a colonial modernity. The myth of the postcolonial state was rooted in the myth of the state itself, as German philosopher Ernst Cassirer detailed it.[10] The collapse of the Pahlavi state therefore is a foregone conclusion when both the first and the second Pahlavis had to be brought to power first by the British and then by the British and American imperial interventions—ascending the peacock throne, pretending they were there since the time of Cyrus the Great.

That central contradiction did not die with the Pahlavi dynasty, and it resurfaced with even more tenacity, coming back to haunt the Islamist regime in the very designation of the idea of an "Islamic republic"—an even more chimeric proposition that was neither

"Islamic" nor a "republic." It has always been this central contradiction that ultimately dismantled its own legitimacy. This contradiction has always been definitive to the calamitous adaptation of a forced postcolonial extension of the colonial logic of the nation-state. An Islamic republic is, as Wael Hallaq rightly says, an impossible state, shoving the moral imagination of a legalistic discourse through the doctrine of Velayat-e Faqih down the throat of not just a republic but a public and its citizenship that is supposed to people that republic. For forty-six years and counting, the Islamic Republic has had to hold itself together by the scaffolding of, first, the US hostage crisis, then the Iran-Iraq War, followed by the aggressive involvement in the geopolitics of the region, from Yemen to Lebanon and Palestine all the way up to Ukraine. Meanwhile, it could not speak to its own citizenry, which was never its own, with any language other than brute force.

This ultimately is the reason why the next Iranian revolution cannot be theorized and scripted except as an afterthought. While the dominant mode of thinking regarding revolutions is and remains statism—reaching for and taking control of the means of state violence—the theorization of what will happen in the course of a revolutionary exercise is an exercise in futility: a tyrannical state will collapse to make room for another tyrannical state. Both the left and the right fighting for elbow room for themselves share in this useless statism. This battle is not based on real differences but on phantom ideologies that have lost their raison d'être. At the epicenter of this battle remains not the state but the public sphere. Neither the shape of the future state nor the political parties that are supposed to bring it about could possibly be rooted in that public sphere. That public sphere is now transnational and includes cyberspace. Against that mass deception of cyberspace, where things are real and unreal at one and the same time, smaller gatherings to protect the agency of the otherwise atomized individuals interrupt the centrality of state, as well as the political parties that might bring it about. A fragmented public sphere is where the battles for the future of any sort of polity are taking place. The next Iranian revolution cannot be theorized because the dominant discourse of statism sustains a false hope in a total and final state to address and resolve all our endemic issues, a bizarre concoction of distant mythologies of salvation and a postmodern gestation of the colonial state. All states are monopolies of violence, as Max Weber observed early in the twentieth century. Reaching out to grasp and control that monopoly of violence is the way we have habitually understood revolutions. Resistance to that state violence and procuring a measure of civic life is a whole different idea of freedom, this time liberated from the delusion of democracy.

THREE

THE REAL PERILS AND THE FALSE PROMISES OF ETHNIC NATIONALISM

After Halabja* suffocated,
I wrote a long complaint to God
Before everyone,
I read it to a tree.
The tree cried.
From one side, a bird, a postman,
Said, "All right, who will deliver it?
If you are expecting me to take it,
I won't reach Gods throne.
Late that night,
My angelic poem, dressed for mourning,
Said, "Don't worry.
I will take it to the heights
Of the atmosphere . . . .
The next day, it was returned.
God's fourth secretary down,
A man by the name of Obaid,

At the bottom
Of the very same complaint,
Wrote to me in Arabic:
"Idiot, make it Arabic.
People here don't know Kurdish.
They won't take it to God."

—Sherko Bekas (1988)

One of the most divisive issues that almost immediately surfaced early in the Zhina uprising was the vexing question of the presumed Kurdish separatism. There were those among Iranian Kurdish activists, by no means all or even representative of any significant constituency, who were vociferously advocating for a separate Kurdish state that would ultimately bring together Kurds of Iran, Iraq, Syria, and Turkey to form one large Kurdish state. To anger Iranian nationalists who were justifiably concerned about the fragmentation of their homeland they insisted that the very idea of "Iran" was entirely fake and that the whole country had to be dismantled. The infamous French Zionist agent provocateur Bernard-Henri Lévy was sympathetic to this cause and was on a rampage advocating for dismantling the territorial integrity of Iran. This separatist faction found receptive and sympatric ears in Israel, Saudi Arabia, and even the United States among the hardcore reactionaries.

This expression of ethnic nationalism in Iran has never been limited to Kurdistan, nor is it a recent development. However, Zhina Mahsa Amini, the young woman who had been arrested by the police and who subsequently died in custody, was Kurdish.

The earliest version of the main slogan of the uprising, "Zan, Zendegi, Azadi" (Women, Life, Freedom), was also believed to have been Kurdish in origin, "Jin, Jiyan, Azadi." There were thus voluble voices at the heart of the Zhina event considering the widespread use of this slogan, the sign of the "colonization" of Kurdish culture and politics. They wanted to claim the trauma of Mahsa Zhina Amini's death, as well as the leading slogan of the uprising, to assert that the slogan and the first martyr were exclusively Kurdish, must remain singularly Kurdish, and anyone suggesting the slightest consideration would be branded a racist, reactionary "Persianist," an agent of the Islamic Republic in disguise, and an altogether fascist.

WHO WOULD BENEFIT FROM FRAGMENTATION OF NATIONS?

A few years ago, in a piece I wrote for Al Jazeera,[1] I observed: Who can blame the Iraqi Kurds for wishing to establish a separate and autonomous state for themselves? Certainly no Iraqi who still cares to remember the murderous history of Saddam Hussein's Anfal genocide and Halabja massacre of the Kurdish population, predicated on a long history of denying their identity and trying to "Arabize" them. Who can blame the Kurds in Iran if they, too, wanted to join forces with their fellow Kurds across the border and form a new country with them? Certainly, no Iranian who cares to recall the slaughter of Kurds early in the course of the Islamic Revolution, and in fact their systematic repression before it—all of that rooted in a ghastly racist history of "Persian supremacy" denigrating the very language and proud culture of the Kurdish people. Who can blame the Kurds in Turkey if they, too, wanted to join Iraqi and Iranian Kurds to form a nation-state of their own? Certainly not Recep Tayyip Erdoğan and his supporters of his brand of Turkish nationalism, with an entire history of the persecution of their own Kurdish population, again trying to deny their history and identity and calling them "Mountain Turks." Who can blame the Syrian Kurds if they, too, wished to join other Kurds and break away from Syria? Certainly no Syrian who still suffers through the bloody regime of Bashar al-Assad and the long and languorous history of denying Kurds their civil liberties and rights.

Indeed: Who can blame any Kurd anywhere in the Arab and Muslim world demanding a state of their own? Certainly no American administration that has historically used and abused the Kurds for their own imperial and strategic purposes, most recently to defeat the Islamic State of Iraq and the Levant (ISIL), and then abandoned them to their own devices when it comes to their wish for independence.

The cause of Kurdish separatism in any country where Kurds currently live is perfectly understandable, but it is alas no cause for celebration in a region already plagued with ethnic nationalism of multiple vintages. The partition and dismantling of four sovereign postcolonial states—Iraq, Syria, Turkey, and Iran—to carve an autonomous Kurdistan (much to the delight of the Israeli settler colony) would be as disastrous for the entirety of the region as it would be for the Kurds themselves. In an alternative scenario, the Kurds remain within these states may be, as they have always been, enormously consequential for the eventual resurrection of pluralistic, tolerant, and cosmopolitan nations. No Iranian, Turk, or Arab can or should even try to pontificate to Kurds about Kurdish independence. Only Kurds themselves can critically think through and act upon their decisions. Generations of Kurdish struggles to secure the dignity of their own collective consciousness have given them the right to do so. It is from within the contexts of those struggles that they need to ask themselves if the racialized ethnic nationalism of their own kind is an answer to the calamitous racialized ethnic chauvinism from which they are justly running away.

Suppose—to Benjamin Netanyahu and the entirety of the Israeli settler colony's utter delight—all these nation-states built around the Kurds completely broke down to all their racialized, ethnicized communities. Instead of Iraq, Iran, Turkey, and Syria as we know them now—all of them multilingual, multicultural, multifaceted mosaics of people plowing through the thick and thin of their shared postcolonial history—we were to have myriad ethnically *pure* Kurdish, *pure* Baluchi, *pure* Arab, *pure* Persian, *pure* Turk, *pure* Turkmen, *pure* Yazidi, *pure* Azeri, ad absurdum ethnic states—on the model of the *"pure* Jews" gathered in Palestine and calling themselves "Israel." What a *pure* fascistic nightmare of the Nazi vintage would that prospect be! Who will benefit from the fragmentation of this Bantustan? Will this potential scenario advance or hinder the cause of peace, justice, "democracy," and prosperity for the people of these fragmentations? What will these fragments have gained; what will have they lost?

I have lost count of how many pieces the bastion of liberal Zionism *Haaretz* has published in support of Kurdish independence—how much ludicrous false solidarity going back all the way to Salah al-Din al-Ayyubi, believe it or not![2] They simply have no shame. But why would this lasting vestige of European colonialism in Palestine be so adamant in its support for an independent Kurdistan? There are many wicked reasons for it but one in particular is important to highlight. The Israeli settler colony is constitutionally discomforted by any pluralistic nation in the region, for it exposes the ethnic racism and unabashed Jewish supremacy at the root of Zionism. The more ethnically fragmented the region in which they live, the paler will appear the European settler colony in their midst. Let the entire Arab and Muslim world break down and fracture into tiny ethnic, xenophobic, racist colonies so "Israel" and its own brand of Jewish supremacy racism feels perfectly at home in Palestine. Divide them to their tiniest racialized denominators so you can rule them better.

Israel, however, is not the only entity opposing that multicultural cosmopolitanism. Every single long-standing ethnic nationalism dominant as a state ideology in the region and their ruling regimes—Arab, Iranian, or Turkish—have historically brutalized the Kurds (along with other populations) in their midst precisely because their rule is so constitutionally illegitimate in face of the truth and reality of that pluralistic cosmopolitanism. But neither the Zionist support for an autonomous Kurdistan nor the anti-Kurdish hysteria opposing it should detract an iota of attention from the fact that a whole history of Kurdish suffering at the hands of these states has given them every moral right to demand and exact a measure of autonomy for themselves. But, and here is the rub, the addition of yet another state-sponsored ethnic nationalism on the model of the four states in which Kurds are located will not be a recipe of political liberation or cultural emancipation. Quite the contrary: it will do precisely the opposite and entrap the Kurds within a smaller gathering inside multiple encampments of religious and ethnic sectarianism in the region. Adding a Kurdish ethnic nationalism to the already metastasized Turkish, Arab, and Iranian chauvinism will turn the entire region even more pronouncedly into the mirror image of the militant sectarianism of the Zionist settler colony.

THE BATTLE FOR AGONISTIC PLURALISM

So, what is the answer? And where should we look for alternatives? The bloody persecution of Iranian Kurds early in the course of the Islamic Revolution in Iran (1977 to 1979) was not because they were all separatists—though even if they were it was their political right. It was because the Iranian Kurdistan had become the cornerstone of a potential revolutionary opposition to the militant Islamists in Tehran brutalizing the revolution toward their sectarian monopoly. That emancipatory politics should always remain the model of Kurdish and all other kinds of political aspirations. If Kurds were to remain where they are and become integral to the transnational liberation movements of their respective countries, by their very presence they will force those states to transform their wretched identity-politics and bourgeois nationalism into emancipatory politics and civic liberties. If they remain and struggle for their own civil liberties, they will liberate their cause from endemic ethnic nationalism and set an example for those with whom they have shared their destiny. If they partition and leave, they will replicate and exacerbate the ethnic racism and bourgeois nationalism from which they are running away. If they stay and fight for their liberty in the company of those around them (Arabs, Iranians, or Turks), they will pivot toward a far more emancipatory future.

In the face of the referendum in Iraqi Kurdistan, for example, one cannot be absolutist, pessimistic, or nihilistic. The alternative to an independent Kurdistan in Iraq cannot and should not be business as usual and the dissolution of Kurdish communal or even national aspirations into the larger frame of dysfunctional or despotic ruling regimes. However justified, Kurdish ethnic nationalism is reactive and reactionary, not proactive and progressive. It plunges the region, Kurds included, further down the rabbit hole of retrograde parochialism, racism, nativism, ethnic nationalism, sectarianism, and hateful jingoism. It is a reaction that the ruling regimes in Iraq, Iran, Syria, and Turkey deserve but that will irreparably damage the future of a political pluralism for Arabs, Iranians, Turks, and Kurds themselves.

It is impossible to consider the question of the Kurds in Iran without a simultaneous attention to their regional predicament. The intensification of Kurdish separatism in Iraq or anywhere else for that matter is a symptom not a cause of the further disintegration of the Arab and Muslim world. If the response to the legitimate desire of Kurds for autonomy is military maneuvers and armed confrontation, the shutting down of water resources, and even more racist anti-Kurdish jingoism, then the dismantling of the current map of the region does not need any help from the Israeli settler colony. Palestinian uprising against the colonial occupation of their homeland is a blueprint for national liberation movements around the globe. As they carved a Zionist settler colony in Palestine, European colonialists could have easily mapped a Kurdistan in the region too. That they did not do so was because of their own colonial interests, not because they harbored any particular dislike for the Kurds. Today, too, the Kurdish aspirations for a homeland, however legitimate they may appear, are impossible to imagine except on the model of the Zionist settler colony that so enthusiastically endorses it, and thousands of Kurds openly and enthusiastically embrace the Israeli flag, the single most hateful sign of European colonialism, racism, and armed thievery in the region.

The political map of every single country in the region today is the result of the encounter between the last Muslim empires— Mughal in India, the Qajars in Iran, and, closest to continental Europe, the Ottomans—confronting French, British, and Russian imperialism in particular. The most psychotic symptom of European imperialism, known as the Sykes–Picot Agreement of 1916, signed between the United Kingdom and France, broke down the Ottoman Empire in a way that would best serve their own interests. The result is the cluster of the current nation-states, in all of which the ruling states are there to facilitate the European and US domination and therefore to repress not to represent the nations on which they have laid a false claim. The addition of yet another repressive nation-state abusing and misrepresenting yet another nation will not solve that historical problem. It will only exacerbate it. The battle for political pluralism must therefore be fought and won from within these very colonial states and the nations they do not represent. In that perfectly plausible aspiration, Kurds and their democratic dreams will travel precisely in the opposite direction of the wishes of the Israeli settler colony and become a model for Europe, which now faces its own separatist movements from Cyprus to Catalonia to Scotland.

The particularity of the Kurdish (or any other so-called minority) question could therefore not have any progressive prospect except on the map of an agonistic pluralism that is definitive to all postcolonial polities.[3] Kurds are integral to an agonistic pluralism right where they are, demanding and exacting their collective rights, not collapsing into any reactionary state formation but affecting pluralistic change in the entirety of the polity they inhabit as a critical ingredient of any and all prospects of liberation from the state violence they all face. As Chantal Mouffe puts it:

> The key thesis of "agonistic pluralis"... [is] that a central task of democratic politics is to provide the institutions which will permit conflicts to take an "agonistic" form, where the opponents are not enemies but adversaries among whom exists a conflictual consensus. What I intended to show with this agonistic model was that it was possible, even when starting with the assertion of the ineradicability of antagonism, to envisage a democratic order.[4]

I borrow that idea without the illusion of any prospect of democratic order, but with full confidence that agonistic pluralism is a condition of a just and equitable polity rather than democratic governance.

INTERNAL AND REGIONAL LABOR MIGRATIONS

Let us now turn to the core of the issue definitive to that agonistic pluralism: dismantling the bourgeois nationalism of all sorts in the region is the fact of internal and regional labor migrations into major cosmopolitan cities of all the countries in the region. A fact that makes a mockery of any and all kinds of "pure" ethnic bourgeois nationalism: Kurdish, Arab, Iranian.

Let me use my own biographical reference to dismantle yet another myth of Arab separatism in southern Iran. I was born and raised in Ahvaz in southern Iran, and I lived there until I graduated from high school in 1969 and went to Tehran to attend college. My father was originally from Bushehr and my mother originally from Dezful—both southern cities. As a young man, my father had come to Ahvaz to work for the Iranian national railroad company, and my maternal grandparents had migrated from Dezful in search of better jobs and brighter futures for their children. My parents married in Ahvaz and I was the middle son of three children they raised. In short, my parents were internal labor immigrants and the offspring of labor immigrants. In our part of the city, near Pol-e Siah (the Black Bridge), we had an Isfahani mosque on one side and an Armenian church on the other, one catering to labor migrants from the city of Isfahan and the other to Armenian families from all over the country. There was also a Bushehri mosque farther away from us that my family and I frequented because my father was an active member of that mosque. The mosque also acted as a base for an impromptu labor union of émigré Bushehris. In these environments, some of my classmates spoke Arabic as their mother tongue while others spoke their Persian with distinctly Shirazi, Dezfuli, Isfahani, or Tabrizi accents.[5] But we were all at home in our hometown, and no one had any exclusive claims on it.

The story of my parents and our neighborhood and my schooling was fairly typical of the demographic composition of Ahvaz and, by extension, the rest of the oil-rich Khuzestan province all the way down to the port cities of Abadan and Khorramshahr. Like the rest of Khuzestan province, Ahvaz, its capital, was a labor immigrant city. Iranians, Arabs, and other labor migrants all the way from Palestine, southern India, and even East Africa all came to Ahvaz, Abadan, or Khorramshahr in search of work, and none of them had any exclusive claim on the city.

I share these details about my early childhood to illustrate the factual diversity of my hometown in which no ethnic nationalist claim (Persianist or Arabist) on this decidedly border city has any shred of legitimacy. The colonial mapping of the world—post-Qajar and post-Ottoman territories included—has crossed many border regions in which the historical fact and force of labor migrations make a mockery of any delusional ethnonationalist claims of one sort or another. Our history is cosmopolitan not by any bourgeois liberal fantasy, but by the bone-deep and bloodied fact of successive and multiple labor migrations. We were united by the toil of our parents' labor, not by the murderous fantasies of any *pure* race. Calling the Persian Ahvaz in its Arabic diction Ahwaz, is a perfectly innocent variation on the same theme. But based on that innocence then claiming the entire province of Khuzestan is "Arabestan" is as delusional as claiming it exclusively for its Persian-speaking populations or any other such designation. There were and there remain many South Indian as East African aspects to that cosmopolitan and multicultural part of Iran as Arab or Persian. This fusion of peoples and their points of origin was no conspiracy by any ruling state. It commenced upstream with commercial conditions that had necessitated successive waves of labor migrations—as indeed to this very day any snapshot of the Persian Gulf area will immediately show you, there is more South Indian, or East African, or Sri Lankan or Filipino presence in that area than Persian and Arab combined—and no amount of racialized ethnonationalism could alter that fact.

Like the rest of West Asia, there are serious structural calamities in every province of Iran, including Khuzestan, Sistan and Baluchistan, and Kurdish regions in the western parts of the country. The incompetence, negligence, and corruption of the central government are chiefly responsible for decades of neglect and therefore accumulated anger. Drinking water in Khuzestan is increasingly scarce; natural resources are being depleted; urban decay is rampant; rates of unemployment among the youth are disproportionately higher in these regions than other parts of the country; a mostly oil-based economy is failing to generate new job opportunities. There are staggering levels of poverty in the Sistan and Baluchistan region that the authorities among the ruling regime have acknowledged. The environment is simply ripe for desperate acts. The slightest manifestation of Arab, Baluch, or Kurdish cultural pride is treated suspiciously and violently repressed. None of these facts justifies state violence. They instead point to endemic problems the ruling state has miserably failed to address. These are serious issues that require serious attention. But ludicrous ethnonationalist ideologies of one sort or another will not resolve such problems and can only exacerbate them further. The ruling regime in Tehran and its counterparts in Riyadh, Abu Dhabi, or Tel Aviv are all equally responsible for the calamitous conditions in which Iranians and Arabs and all other communities around them find themselves across the region. Iran is a multicultural, multiethnic, and multilingual country, reminiscent of its own imperial past and its later colonially conditioned borders. There is no such race as Persian. Period. Persian is a language, not a race—and Iranians speak it with varieties of accents right next to their mother tongues, whether Arabic or Turkish. What has united them is not any racist "Persian" central government. What has united them is their collective struggle for liberty. Collectively they are the majority—none of them any minority against the "Persian majority," which is a total fiction. The only "minority" is the ruling state that has never fully represented them.

CENTRIPETAL NATIONALISM
AND CENTRIFUGAL SOCIALISM

When the myth of the postcolonial state—from the Pahlavis to the
Islamic Republic—is exposed for the sad and bitter tale that it is,
we are back to the earliest periods of the Constitutional Revolution
early in the twentieth century, when in the midst of superpower
rivalries between the Russians and the British the idea of Iran as a
postcolonial nation-state, rooted in its own imperial past, was taking shape and when the interface between a centripetal bourgeois
nationalism and a constellation of centrifugal socialist movements
defined the political disposition of the country. As in the first quarter of the twentieth century, Reza Shah was getting ready to mount
his UK-sponsored military coup, ideologically charged by a deep-
rooted bourgeois nationalism at the center of Tehran; meanwhile,
socialist uprisings, supported by the newly active Soviet imperialism, were fomenting in areas ranging from Azerbaijan to Gilan and
Mazandaran. That dynamic, a sign of political health and moral
imagination, has defined much of twentieth-century Iranian history and continued apace, except, now, the totality of it has disin-
tegrated into multiple ethnic nationalisms—particularly evident
in Kurdish, Turkish, Baluch, and Arab regions. The only way this
historic fact has played itself out in progressive terms is through
the agonistic pluralism of both bourgeois nationalism and peripheral socialism working against each other inside a unified polity
that sustains itself dialectically. Otherwise, we have the metastasis
of the most pernicious ethnic nationalism replicating bourgeois
nationalism from which they are running away.

In a general panorama of the postcolonial history of Iran, we
might say bourgeois nationalism was always gravitating toward

the capital Tehran, and socialist tendencies were pulling away and toward the provinces. The movement led by Mirza Kuchak Khan Jangali in Gilan was a prime example of such centripetal movements, against which Reza Shah represented a bourgeois nationalism that colonial interests obviously preferred, while the centripetal socialist forces were inspired by the Russian example, which the Soviet Union endorsed and supported. When they failed in their aspirations, the socialist tendencies on the peripheries of the nation eventually degenerated into ethnic nationalism replicating the center. In its healthiest mode these forces have been agonistic and complementary, and in the sickest form antagonistic and separatist. Today both these elements exist: a healthy socialism and a sick ethnic nationalism that carries the fragmented memories of their past. Israel and Saudi Arabia and even the United States want to take advantage of this fragmented condition—the same way that the US, UK, and Soviet imperial machinations were also at play when Azerbaijan, Kurdistan, Khuzestan, Baluchistan, Gilan, Mazandaran, and Khorasan were all subject to socialist aspirations. A divisive character like Seyyed Ja'far Pishevari (1892–1947) in Azerbaijan; a straightforward colonial agent ethnic separatist like Sheikh Khaz'al (1863–1936) in Khuzestan; and a revolutionary figure like Mirza Kuchak Khan Jangali (1880–1921) in Gilan were all part of this scene.

If we were to pull back from the regional scene and look at the matter from the perspective of the global refugee crisis, the conditions of the Kurds and other people from war-torn areas have not been well in the United States, Europe, and elsewhere where they have been put in a paradoxical position. When they seek asylum and refugee status and citizenship in other countries they are advocating for open borders and hospitable multiculturalism, and yet when it comes to their demands for a separate country for themselves they become ultranationalist, advocating for an independent Kurdistan with solid borders. This is what we see in a figure like Behrouz Boochani, the award-winning journalist whose account of refugee life in the Australian-run Manus Island detention center in Papua New Guinea, *No Friend But the Mountains* (2018), was justly celebrated around the globe. Yet, when he joined the Zhina uprising, an ultra-Kurdish nationalist suddenly surfaced in him. Since the rise of the Zhina uprising Boochani has been a vociferous ethnic nationalist for whom everything begins and ends with the Kurds, much on the same model that for a white supremacist their identity centers around the British, American, or Australian label, or how, for a Zionist in Palestine, their ethnicity defines the tall walls they wish to build around themselves. The same walls Boochani and his fellow ethnonationalists wish to build around their Kurdistan with Israeli and Kurdish flags hoisted next to each other and NATO bombs helping them create yet another ethnic enclave. That this kind of ethnic nationalism is akin to Nazism, or white supremacy, replicated in settler colonial Zionism and militant Hinduism does not seem to bother militant Kurdish, Turkish, Baluch, or Arab nationalists, that they have become their own enemies and are running toward that from which they think they are running away.

In the context of postcolonial nations proper, though, the paradox of these centrifugal movements is that if they stay within the agonistic system of their pluralistic society they are adding a significant socialist force to it, and if they leave it behind they degenerate into a replica of the bourgeois nationalism they wish to leave behind. There is a constitutive pluralism in all postcolonial states, where ethnicized minorities and ethnicized majorities have had to negotiate a coexistence. There is no metanarrative that could bring them together otherwise. Political conflict is inevitable. But contrary to some theorists of agonistic pluralism, this state is not tragic—it is actually quite a blessing. Kurds, or Turks, or Baluchis, or the so-called Persians, as constituencies of a collective polity, can have primary relations within themselves and secondary citizenship duties toward each other. A Kurd or a Baluch may like their mother tongue and their father's cooking better than any other. But they are also integral to a larger polity that is not reducible to one's mother tongue or the measure of salt, pepper, and turmeric they like in their dishes. That pluralism defines the nation from which a corresponding state may or may never rise. It is only the totalitarian disposition of the ruling states that has translated into a totalizing narrative of the nations they have never fully represented, whereas harmonious or even conflictual relationships among the classes and communities of a nation are both evident and indeed a blessing. Left to their own devices, as a Gesellschaft (society), a nation can and should consist of multiple Gemeinschafts (communities).

THE NATION AND ITS FRAGMENTS

A postcolonial nation by definition is not mono-ethnic and could not possibly be mono-ethnic. The carving out of multiple Muslim empires from the Mughals to the Qajars to the Ottomans by European colonial powers has created a quilt of multiethnic polities. Postcolonial nations have therefore come to be by virtue of a collectivity of resistance to European colonial domination of the earth. Moreover, postcolonial nations like those in India, Iran, Turkey, or Egypt carry the distant memories of their own imperial pasts, which were by definition multiethnic. From two opposing ends of history therefore—their imperial pasts and their colonial encounters with Europe—postcolonial nations are multiethnic, both in roots and in their purposeful politics. Postcolonial nations therefore face myriad issues that will not be addressed but are in fact multiplied by addition of one or more ethnic nationalisms to them.

Against that dreadful prospect, we have the factual evidence of multiethnic pluralism that has historically defined the very ideas of the nation in the region. In Partha Chatterjee's seminal study, *The Nation and Its Fragments: Colonial and Postcolonial Histories* (1993), he considers that the nationalist imagination on colonial sites in Asia and Africa have been posited not on *identity* but on *difference*. He makes a distinction between anticolonial nationalism and nationalism as a political ideology of state-building, for the former has a much more robust and productive domain than the latter. Crucially, Chatterjee assigns the question of sovereignty to anticolonial nationalism. In the battle between political nationalism and colonialism, the powers of the nation have been violently appropriated by ideological forces of state-building. Chatterjee also makes a distinction between what he calls the material and spiritual spheres of nationalism, and he makes the crucial argument that the nation was first imagined in spiritual and not territorial terms. Chatterjee makes a gentle but strong objection to Benedict Anderson's idea of nations as "imagined communities" from a decidedly postcolonial standpoint, positing anticolonial nationalism as his modus operandi.[6] What we see in Asia and Africa is not based on identity but on difference, not just with the colonial model but within itself. We are part of a nation not by virtue of our abstract similarities but by virtue of our marked differences on a common collective history. Chatterjee therefore objects that nationalism should be taken as a mere political movement, for it is also a condition of being. In my language, I make a similar distinction between nationalism as an ideology of state-building and the idea of the nation predicated on anticolonial struggles and therefore the predicate of a social movement formed obviously in opposition both to European colonialism and domestic tyrannies it had occasioned and enabled. Nations as a political force can therefore be against nationalism as a state ideology.

It is in that context that the history of anticolonial struggles has created a robust conception of the nation in which agonistic pluralism is definitive to its very historic origins. From the fragments of former empires, and in confrontation with the colonial conquest of the world, fragmented national polities have emerged, each consisting of multiple ethnicities, races, and genders. This at its heart is the strength and power of these national entities, protecting them from the terror of ethnic racism of the sort that has been definitive to the Israeli settler colony and now a terror to all democratic claims from the United States and its evangelical racism to India and its Hindu fanaticism to Iran and its militant Islamism.

FOUR

KHIZESH AS INTIFADA
AT LARGE

*Chaos never descends upon a house abruptly. First a
gentle dust sits between the cracks of wooden panels, in
between the folded layers of bedsheets, inside the cracks
of windows, and hiding in the waves of the hanging
curtains, waiting for a wind that would blow through an
open door of the house and liberate the fragmented pieces
from their hideouts.*

—**Ghazaleh Alizadeh** (1991)

Over the last decade, between 2010 and 2021, I have published
six books on the idea of the Intifada. These six books, when considered together—preferably in chronological order—form a particular strand of thought woven through all of my work, and that
mode of thinking informs my thoughts on the Zhina uprising.[1] My
approach to Intifada is informed and inspired by the Palestinian
idea and practice, but it is not limited to that domain or confined to
Palestinian struggles. I extend the idea of Intifada from a specific

historical origin to its potential larger theoretical implications. There are particularities to the Zhina uprising of 2022 to 2023 that I have sought to identify and detail in this book, yet that specificity must be understood in more regional and global terms than Iran itself. The term that best describes the Zhina uprising is the Persian word "Khizesh," which we might consider the functional equivalent of "Intifada," though the difference between the two Persian and Arabic words might also help us understand both better.

FROM INTIFADA TO KHIZESH: REVOLUTIONS WITHOUT ENDS

I have used the word Intifada in my series of books inspired by the Palestinian uprisings against the colonial armed robbery of their homeland, though not just in the Palestinian sense of the term, but in a larger sense in the spirit of their articulation of a different mode of resistance to tyranny, of a politics of defiance, of being political on a permanent basis and as a state of being, which I have in turn moved into a theoretical domain with a decidedly epistemological challenge to the Eurocentric disciplinary thinking we have all inherited from the conditions of our violent coloniality. The word "Intifada" here defines a particular mode of political and theoretical resistance to colonial and patriarchal thinking in which we have habitually thought about our place in history. The "Intifada" mood is neither social-scientific nor humanist in the disciplinary senses we have inherited and inhabited—and yet it partakes in both of them selectively and purposefully. It allows for the lived experiences of Palestinians under occupation of a settler colony to inform a particular kind of political and theoretical articulation—a specific kind of revolt. It is crucial to keep in mind that there is no English, French, German, Italian, or any other linguistic equivalent to Intifada, and we must continue to use it in its original Palestinian Arabic. Words such as "rebellion" or "uprising" or a "resistance movement" come close to it but do not completely comprehend it. The etymological root of the word is "tremor," "shivering," "shuddering"—all implied in the Arabic term "nafada" meaning "to shake," "to shake off," or "to get rid of." This etymology better helps us grasp the meaning of the word. But there always remains a crucial differential between the original Palestinian term Intifada and even how other Arabs may understand the word.

In Persian, the word we have used for the Zhina uprising is "Khizesh"—an equally compelling word rooted in related ideas of "jumping," "rising," "revolting," but also "insurrection" and even "resurrection." It is a much different word from "Enqelab," which means "revolution." The Palestinian Intifada and the Persian Khizesh are almost identical in their connotations—though the word Intifada has now become a global signifier with which we might also understand the Khizesh-e Zhina. What is common to both Intifada and Khizesh is that they are revolutionary in posture but not revolutions in the classical sense of the term— for which we have "Thawra" in Arabic and "Enqelab" in Persian. Revolutions intend to dismantle the ruling state and replace it with another. The Pahlavi monarchists are adamant in calling the Zhina uprising a revolution, for they wish to overthrow the Islamic Republic and replace it with a Pahlavi monarchy, the same way that the Islamic Republic confiscated the Iranian Revolution of 1977 to 1979 and overthrew the Pahlavis. But Intifada and Khizesh neither intend to nor are they satisfied with the overthrow of the ruling regime so far as another tyrannical claim to

democracy is waiting and poised to replace it. The Palestinian
Intifada is not just against Israel, it is equally against a corrupt
Palestinian leadership and other Arab leaders too. It is a state of
being for Palestinians. The same is true about Khizesh-e Zhina.
Its goal is not just to morally and imaginatively dismantle and
overthrow the Islamic theocracy. It has also pulled the rug from
under the throne of the next tyrant—Reza Pahlavi, Maryam
Rajavi, or the disgraced Islamophobe (and Aung-San-Suu-Kyi-
wannabe) Masih "the Charlatan" Alinejad, a career opportunist
agent provocateur who is a pure fabrication of the US media.

I also look at the events of Iran of 2022 to 2023 mindful of the
specificities of its unfolding in its own immediate historical context and yet in terms of a kind of *il pensiero debole* (weak thought),
as articulated by Italian philosopher Gianni Vattimo.[2] *Il pensiero
debole* refers to a mode of thinking, knowing, and being that lacks
foundational epistemologies, which is what I believe the Intifada or
Khizesh mode of resistance to tyranny to be, both in the political
and theoretical sense.[3] It is a simultaneous critique of both metaphysics and ideology. While the former critique, more metaphysical, is deeply indebted to Vattimo's engagement and parts ways
with Heidegger, the latter is rooted in his detailed reading of mundane realities suspended from any ideological formations—for or
against the state. Weak thought, therefore, is poised, in both its
metaphysical and ideological ambitions, against any assumptions
of totality, closure, and terminations.[4] In this way of thinking, Vattimo suspends the Heideggerian formation of Being, or *Dasein*, in
the interests of the more palpable and unphilosophical beings—of
which he then makes a philosophical proposition.[5] "The enfeeble-
ment of (the notion of) Being . . . has serious repercussions for the
way we conceive of thinking and of the *Dasein* that is its 'subject,'"

he concludes. "Weak thought aims at articulating such repercussions and thereby preparing a new ontology."[6] In the domain of that weak ontology that is Vattimo's philosophical project, human being, human thinking, and human purposes are not nor could they ever be teleological, total, definitive, final, or deterministic. The terror and joy of being is precisely in its indeterminant contingency, which is the contingency of the revolutionary state I detect and propose in the Zhina uprising, as opposed to the revolutionary ideologies of one sort or another that may lay a false and tenuous claim on it. *Il pensiero debole* therefore enables us to think of Zhina not as a revolution but as revolutionary state, a Khizesh.

The books that I wrote on the Intifada mode of thinking, based on these philosophical and political predicates, are rooted in my more academic thinking and scholarly writings at large, but they address the wider global public in terms of our political hopes and despairs. In retrospect, these books began with my detailed reading of Iran's Green Movement (2009 to 2010) as a major moment of an epistemic shift in the geopolitics of the region, where I proposed a different kind of thinking about such social uprisings. I then proposed a critical reading of the role of "native informers"— comparator intellectuals in the function of US imperialism—when and where émigré intellectuals become rootless misinformers and ideological guns for hire. In the third volume, I offered one of the earlier critical readings of the Arab revolutions of 2010 to 2011 as a stage where we were liberated from the political delusions of the postcolonial state as one form of totalizing thinking. In the fourth installment I made a decidedly rhetorical move to wonder what the terms of an epistemic rupture would look like if we were to decenter "Europe" as the ontological essence of our reading the world. In the fifth volume I examined the moral and discursive shadows of the condition of European coloniality. And finally, in the sixth and signature volume of this series, I dismantled the false link between nations and their states to liberate the normative foregrounding of our "liberation geography." What we are witnessing in the Iran of 2022 to 2023, the subject of this seventh book in the series, could therefore be read as an extension of this liberation geography where the myth of the postcolonial state has finally imploded and the rise of a new revolutionary politics has now manifested itself as a *state* of being, refusing to yield to any ideology for the next state.

In these successive volumes I have sought to place the postcolonial knowing subject on a transnational public sphere, beyond the colonial divides of "the West and the Rest" or even on the fabricated frontiers of one nation-state as opposed to another, and thus to locate it in the middle of the lived experiences of colonial, anticolonial, and postcolonial epistemic horizons we have received from previous generations of critical thinkers—from Aimé Césaire and Frantz Fanon to Edward Said and Gayatri Spivak. Seminal in the theoretical underpinnings of my project in these books have been the philosophical works of V. Y. Mudimbe from the Democratic Republic of the Congo, Enrique Dussel from Argentina, and Kojin Karatani from Japan.[7] The enduring task of reading these books in the Intifada series together, and seeing through their collective projects, will remain for future generations of critical thinkers—but at this point I think it is perhaps useful to place my reading of the Zhina uprising in the context of a major epistemic shift in this Intifada series. Reading the Zan, Zendegi, Azadi uprising as an Intifada or Khizesh at large entails a kind of epistemic fluidity that suspends the longevity of civilizational frameworks or national polities on the contingency of a radical contemporaneity, in anticipation of a theorization of any kind of colonial modernity in Iran or elsewhere that has been at odds with all forms of state violence compromising its fruitful unfolding. Suspending the cliché project of revolutions in pursuit of a more democratic state is the most immediate aspect of this new way of thinking of postcolonial politics.

If we were to bring the Intifada/Khizesh thinking and the *il pensiero debole* together, an event like the Zhina uprising posits itself as a suspended moment—an *event,* as Alain Badiou would say—when there is no specific futurity in the chronological sense to which we are progressing, or from which we are parting ways. The moment itself is the fulfillment of all that has happened before it. Liberation here trumps any promise of delivery toward democracy, whether claimed by the ruling theocracy or promised by the pestiferous monarchy it overcame and that now wants its throne back. Everything today is where things are supposed to be—at the commencement of the Zhina uprising, which is also its own conclusion. The state has effectively collapsed and has no moral or political authority. The Islamic Republic is dead, as one graffiti on a wall put it succinctly, except it does not know it yet. People are liberated from any delusion of delivery, of any promised land, especially those promised by the cultic mojahedin or defeated monarchists. Iranian citizens live with the ruling regime like Palestinians do with the Zionist occupying forces. They live as they do their best to dodge their bullets and bombs, security forces, and spying agencies. Yes, the ruling regime harasses them, arrests them, point-blank maims and murders them, destroys their environment, and wastes their national resources. In short, the ruling regime has given it all it has, short of massacring the population in the thousands—as Israelis regularly do in Gaza and the rest of Palestine—of which it is still perfectly capable. But the state of suspension of beliefs itself is a triumphant moment. All the opposition forces are exposed for what they are—pathetic and useless. Even the nostalgia for the Pahlavis does not quite translate to support for his son but instead helps further discredit the Islamist theocracy. If we step back and look at all those unfolding events, we experience a sense of triumphant relief. The society is functioning or lacking and lagging entirely despite the dysfunctional state. Intifada or Khizesh has become permanent, a state of being, a triumphant recognition of the futility and criminality of not just this but all states.

During the Turkish elections in May 2023, I observed the cliché illusion of democracy there with a sense of relief, for there was no such deception left in Iran. All was naked in the Islamic Republic. A ruling Vali Fiqh, a Shah waiting to return to rule, and a President Maryam Rajavi lost in her cultic delirium. All at the same time laying a ludicrous claim on the nation that had rejected them all and deemed them all of illegitimate. In Turkey, if you were to read the racist European press you would wish for victory for Recep Tayyip Erdoğan. If you were to look at the horrid tyrannies from Egypt to Syria, Turkey appeared as God's gift to humanity, and if you were to think of Turkish people, you would think they deserve better than Erdoğan. In Iran, everything was in the open, the vicious ruling Islamist theocracy fully exposed, the defiant nation rebellious, the Rajavi cult insular, the fascism of the Pahlavis fully staged, the charlatanism of bought-and-paid-for opposition puppets like Masih Alinejad fully documented, the Reform Movement dead, the Green Movement just a memory. All that remained was the innocence of the young victims of the regime— Nika Shakarami, Kian Pirfalak, Mahsa Zhina Amini, and many others. This was now an epic battle between good and evil, the beautiful and the ugly, truth and falsehood, as if we were all living through the stories of Ferdowsi's *Shahnameh*—with no illusion of any Islamic democracy or Pahlavi secularism, for we were cured of both. We were at ground zero of a different historical imagination. Thus understood, Khizesh as Intifada is a permanent state of uprising. It is not a revolution toward an end—it is a revolt to disrupt and dismantle the ideological operation of the ruling state, this or any other. With Palestine or Iran as is its epicenter, it moves around the region and even the world. It is not a sudden incident to be analyzed and televised or tweeted, but a permanent revolt that has become a way of life, it is an *il pensiero debole,* and the post-democratic world it announces is more purposeful and meaningful than disappointing or a cul-de-sac. We are not waiting for the regime to collapse, for the regime has already collapsed, and it is held together with the clumsy scaffolding of pure and wanton violence. As such, the Zhina uprising reveals a revolutionary *state,* not a revolution, for there is no messiah to come, no Mahdi, no liberator, except the fake and media-manufactured liberators the internet makes and breaks almost at the same time. A US-media-manufactured hack named Masih Alinejad, with her rank charlatanism, is the poster child of these false messiahs. Like a magnet she attracts the worst and the most corrupt—from Mike Pompeo to Bernard-Henri Lévy—to her careerism. The Zhina uprising, therefore, paradoxically both anticipates and dismantles the promise of the coming revolution. It works through an always "delayed defiance." It is always defiant, and it is always delayed. It celebrates the revolutionary *now* without hoping for a revolution *then*—for that which is supposed to have happened has already happened, the active liberation from the illusion of a democratic postcolonial state.

If chaos, as the opening sentence of Ghazaleh Alizadeh's signature novel, *The House of the Idrisis* (1991), suggests, is not sudden then neither is the rise of a permanent revolutionary state, a sense of revolution without means or ends, a state that will never resolve itself, fail, or succeed. If all Israelis packed their belongings and left for Europe or the United States tomorrow, if the ruling regime in Iran collapsed the same day, there would be no post-Intifada or post-Khizesh state that would come and resolve all the issues left behind. That was and remains a delusion. Colonial and postcolonial states—Israel and the Islamic Republic alike—are the source of calamity, not inspirations for truth and justice. We are delivered from that false prophecy. The Qajars were worse than the Pahlavis. The authoritarian Pahlavi monarchy paved the way for the totalitarian Islamist theocracy, and the Islamist theocracy can only lead to a regime even worse than all the preceding regimes put together. We must conceptually, ideally, emotionally, epistemically, imaginatively abandon all hopes and all trust in any legitimate state. The revolution that is supposed to deliver us is already here. We just need to open our eyes and see and greet it.

THE CHIMERA: A MONARCHIC REPUBLIC CHASING AFTER AN ISLAMIC REPUBLIC

As the sign and signature of staccato uprisings, Intifada is both specific to Palestine and universal to our postcolonial history. With the Persian word Khizesh, we might specify Intifada to the Iranian scene of the Zhina uprising. Intifada is therefore both a spontaneous political act and yet carries a historical memory of struggle from one generation to another. You might say Palestinians have been engaged in an Intifada from the very first day of their colonized history. When the Arab revolutions started, I wrote a piece in which I argued we might consider them "the commencement of the Third Intifada on a transnational, pan-Arab, and pan-Muslim scale."[8] If so, this paradox of memory and forgetfulness becomes dialectical to our understanding of any history of revolt in or out of Palestine, in or out of the Arab and Muslim world. But what would such a consideration of the Zhina uprising as a case of Intifada or Khizesh mean in terms of the political consequences of these events?

A popular essay about the expat opposition during the Zhina uprising is called "Savari Nahamvar bar Tark-e Do Asb-e Baldar" (A Rough Rider on the Back of Two Winged Horses) (2023) by Khosrow Parsa.[9] This brief but poignant essay is about the short-lived coalition of a few Iranian "celebrities" who gathered around Reza Pahlavi, the elder son of the last Pahlavi monarch, as a "coalition" to help bring down the Islamic Republic. This essay was one among many analyses of the short-lived attempted coalition that drew much attention among the Iranian diaspora. The piece begins with a recollection of how Reza Shah (1878–1944), the founder of the Pahlavi dynasty and the grandfather of Reza Pahlavi, came to power with the help of the British. Parsa reminds his readers that Reza Shah, too, was playing the two horses of republicanism and monarchy together. Like his grandfather, Reza Pahlavi, this time based in Washington, DC, dillydallied on what to call himself and on what platform to run to become a king! He declared himself the king soon after his father died in Cairo in July 1980, then he called himself the prince, then again the king, and now, during the Zhina uprising, just a "representative" or "vakil," but then again the king. The author of the essay makes a poignant distinction between the leading elite of the former Pahlavi regime, who ran away with millions and lead comfortable lives abroad, and those who are nostalgic for the old regime. He then turns to some people who had initially gathered around Reza Pahlavi—people like Hamed Esmaeilion, who lost his family in the Ukrainian airliner crash in January 2020 in Iran; Nazanin Boniadi, a Hollywood actress; Masih Alinejad, a bold careerist propped up by the US media; Abdullah Mohtadi, a Kurdish political leader; Shirin Ebadi, a Nobel laureate for peace; Golshifteh Farahani, another actress, but based in Paris; and Ali Karimi, a widely popular footballer. The coalition did not last, for Reza Pahlavi treated these odd people like his own Cabinet in exile—except none of them had any talent besides acting, in the varied sense of the word—so they were quickly dispensed with, and the coalition disbanded. The monarchists tried another strategy: asking people to give him *Vekalat*, or power of attorney, which also became an embarrassment. The turnout was so slow that even his own supporters, like Homa Sarshar, a Los Angeles–based journalist, thought it was a plot by the Islamic Republic to discredit Reza Pahlavi. That fiasco was followed by trying to write a *Manshur*, or a declaration, which was again a joke. This whole sad episode exposed the fragility and vacuity of the opposition, which was divided between the deeply discredited cult of the mojahedin, the emerging delusional cult of the Pahlavis, and the openly bought-and-paid-for regime changers of all sorts wasting American taxpayers' money. A sad spectacle, but ultimately a crucial acid test to see how the expat opposition was a lost cause.

Parsa's short but popular essay, and the ridiculous attempt at coalition building that it exposed, captured the fragmentation of the so-called opposition to the Islamist theocracy outside Iran, a fragmentation that reflected the very spirit of an Iranian political culture in which systematic opposition—predicated on party politics, coalition building, and, above all, a clear conception of what sort of a political future they preferred—was entirely absent. This fragmentation was partially the result of the tyrannical ruling regime in Iran that had systematically destroyed all its legitimate alternatives, either by making them subservient to its whims like the discredited Reformists; silenced and murdered them in its dungeons; or forced them into exile and thus altogether discredited their project. The Islamic Republic was therefore first and foremost responsible for this sad state of affairs. As a brutal and astonishingly violent tyranny, the Islamic Republic had spent over four decades destroying its legitimate alternatives, and this ludicrous spectacle around Reza Pahlavi was perfect evidence of it. But this does not mean the Pahlavi regime before it was a flower bed of democratic institutions. The Shah, too, had established a single party, the Rastakhiz Party, that was under his thumb—and anyone who disagreed with the one-party system was told to leave the country. Neither the Pahlavi regime, therefore, nor the Islamist theocracy that followed it, had any claim to democratic representation or institution building. Like the regime it had succeeded, the Islamic Republic (a contradiction in terms) was a deeply troubled and thoroughly discredited ruling regime. The oscillation of Reza Pahlavi between republicanism and monarchy (on the model of his grandfather) reflected and reciprocated the bizarre republican claims of the Islamic theocracy he opposed and that had an equally nonsensical claim to democratic (republican) representations. The future of Iranian politics could not possibly be imagined outside such a chimeric construct as an Islamic republic or a republican monarchy of the sort the Pahlavi claimant was preaching to his choir.

Like the Chimera in Greek mythology, a fire-breathing hybrid creature usually depicted as a lion with the head of a goat protruding from its back and a tail that looks like a snake, the postcolonial state that appeared first as a rootless Pahlavi mon-

archy and then as an Islamist theocracy is a strange monstros-
ity. The lived experiences of people in such fractured polities is
that the postcolonial state is a polity in search of an archetype it
lacks and that does not exist. The postcolonial state thus mimics
the modernity of a republic, but the coloniality of the condition
through which it has reached that mockery makes it impossible to
lay a solid claim on any such modernity. Two archaic prototypes,
the king and the cleric (or the Shah and the Sheikh, as we might
say) have emerged as the enduring archetypes of political legitimacy, with flawed claims on an impossible democratic state. The
history of "modern" Iran, like the history of any other country
like it, is the history of a nation in search of a political archetype
outside its colonial predicament and yet equally liberated from
the wild-goose chase of "authenticity." This search has proven to
be futile. The result is the surfacing of archaic prototypes like the
Shah and the Sheikh, with dubious claims on people's credulities.
The political circumstances of the nation have hitherto failed to
procure its own archetypal legitimacy. For that reason, the troubled histories of our countries are defined far more accurately by
destabilizing uprisings than by stabilizing states and their fraught
claims to democratic legitimacy. The idea of Khizesh, like Intifada, has a far more solid claim on Iranian political culture than
any other concept ranging from legitimate state to democratic
revolutions. All revolutionary episodes have been Khizesh, or
uprisings kidnapped by one of those archetypes, from the Constitutional Revolution of 1906 to 1911, which was kidnapped by
the Pahlavi monarchy, to the 1977 to 1979 revolution usurped by
the Islamic Republic, down to the Zhina uprising that so far has
refused to yield to the lost aura of the Pahlavi monarchy. These
are not revolutions in search of any enduring democratic states,

but mere uprisings, or Khizesh, or Intifada, in search of an archetype, which cannot be a modern state, for that modernity is a colonial impossibility. That archetype is the idea of the Khizesh, Intifada, itself.

Two cases of Khizesh might be helpful to consider here—one longer in duration and the other much shorter. One is the Jangal uprising early in the twentieth century and the other the Siahkal incident early in the 1970s. If we were to consider these two examples as variations on the theme of Khizesh, they help in our understanding of the sustained history of uprising as a better measure of the political culture that informs these specific events. Led by Mirza Kuchak Khan Jangali (1880–1921), the Jangal Movement in Gilan was a rebellion against the monarchist rule of Reza Shah that lasted from 1915 to 1921. It was a socialist uprising launched against the bourgeois nationalism of the central state that Reza Shah had championed—a bourgeois nationalism that ultimately cost him his throne when the first Pahlavi monarch expressed sympathies for Nazi Germany. The Siahkal uprising of February 8, 1971, in the Siahkal regions of the selfsame Gilan province, was another crucial event that was led by members of the Organization of Iranian People's Fedai Guerrillas. It was instantly crushed and did not get anywhere, yet it triggered the revolutionary momentum that finally led to the Iranian Revolution of 1977 to 1979. We are far better off thinking of the postcolonial history of Iran in terms of such events, which we we might collectively call Khizesh, of shorter or longer durations, minor or major consequences, rather than the two paramount examples of the Constitutional Revolution and the Iranian Revolution, which were usurped by a bourgeois nationalism and a militant Islamism, respectively. The history of democratic uprisings in Iran could be seen either in terms of the chimeric disposition of the failed tyrannical states to which they have led or else in terms of the uprisings themselves; Khizesh or Intifada give us a better sense of the sort of political thinking we might consider for the future and enduring impacts of such uprisings.

The failure to understand the dynamics of the successive crescendos of Khizesh as a logic reflecting the internal dynamics of a postcolonial national history and carrying the active memories of an imperial past has led to casual and amateurish suggestions that Iran has a "long history but a short-termed society."[10] This is a bizarre and oxymoronic proposition, particularly when compared to European societies that are thus presumed to have "long-term societies"—whatever that outlandish idea may mean. Such rough-and-tumble remarks are a clear indication of a deeply colonized and Eurocentric imagination that considers Europe the measure of totalizing historical narratives, and they approximate Iranian or any other national history to what they imagine to have happened in a mythic "Europe" and find it wanting.[11] No society is either long-term or short-term "by nature," except through a self-Orientalizing prose and politics that think a Windsor royal family living through history like parasites is a good thing and that the Pahlavis collapsing in comparison is a bad thing. Would things have been better if the Qajars or the Pahlavis or now the Islamic Republic sustained a "long-term society"? The sheer reactionary implication of the phrase should make one wonder. Iran has had its long dynastic rules with mixed legacy—and what has animated its history is periodic revolts, not "short-term society." These kinds of off-the-cuff remarks are clear indications of a dilettantism, taking liberty with the sustained course of struggles of a nation, enabled by superficial exposures to social sciences and humanities. But more importantly, this kind of cavalier dilettantism betrays a prose and a corresponding politics that systematically disregard the brutal history of (British and other European) colonialism, which is chiefly responsible for seeking to dismantle the organicity of the political cultures they conquered and destroyed. They used to articulate such condescending attitudes by their own colonial officers and Orientalists, and they now speak them through the natives they have trained in their colonial dictions. Beyond the reach of such deliberate distortions of colonial experience and postcolonial thinking, Khizesh in Iran or Intifada in Palestine are the living pulses of wholesome and robust national organisms far healthier in their pulsating recurrences and the spontaneity of their shaking the foundations of tyranny.

THE CASE AGAINST DEMOCRACY

My critique of democracy as a troubled colonial proposition should not be confused with the current rejection of democracy in its European or American domains. Critique of democracy as an institution is nothing new or unusual. Jason Brennan's *Against Democracy* (2017), for example, is mostly read for its dismantling of the cherished myth of democracy where it is claimed most loudly. "Democracy is the rule of the ignorant and the irrational," he proposes, and then argues for what he calls "epistocracy"![12] This is the rule of the so-called knowledgeable. But who is to decide what is the nature of this "knowledge" to be had? This kind of elitist argument is geared more toward the consolidation of the status quo rather than dismantling the trust in the efficacy of the democratic process. The result is a kind of elitist gerrymandering of knowledge production conducive to a democratic claim on polity. Brennan does not fault the system but discredits the voters who are (in his estimation) ignorant and threaten the whole system. He wants voters to be tested, as it were, for knowledge and competence, before they are given voting rights. Epistocracy is, as a result, a better system, he believes, than democracy!

My criticism of democracy as a colonial construct has an entirely different genealogy and purpose. On the model of Intifada in Palestine or the consistency of Khizesh in Iranian political history of the last two centuries, I believe abandoning the illusion of the postcolonial state, which is my argument here, sets our political culture free. My principal proposition, as I reflect on the Zhina uprising of 2022 to 2023, is as follows: postcolonial states like the ruling Islamist regime in Iran have all lost all legitimacy and become total killing machines, without any enduring sense of state sovereignty; in tandem, the nations subject to their tyrannies have been liberated from the phantasmagoric conceptions of democracy staged every few years as public entertainment. The Zhina uprising in Iran has sustained a revolutionary momentum as a Khizesh, not because of the articulated vision of a post-Islamist state that it wants but because of the total rejection of the very idea of the state it has known since the Constitutional Revolution. With the massive popularity of Donald Trump and other similar real or potential tyrants, the illusion of a stable democracy has finally disappeared in the country with the oldest claim to it—and with it the prospect of the United States or any European country offering their versions of "liberal democracies" as a model for the rest of the world to follow. The coincidence of Trump and COVID-19 achieved two things simultaneously: liberated us from the delusion of democracy and forced us into a deep and mandatory look inside. Not liberal democracy but radical, anarchic, subversive uprisings with no clear democratic outlook now define our age. The revolt against mandatory veiling in Iran is the revolt against the totalizing state; against the last revolutionary state created by the pernicious condition of coloniality; and against any totalizing revolutionary narrative that might seek to come after it. This is not to say that any number of reactionary and "secular" claims to the state may not follow after the Islamic Republic, including a military coup of one sort or another, but to mark the fact that the condition of the postcolonial state has now completely exhausted the possibility of even any assumption of a legitimate state. With that fact, so has ended any claim to a total revolution that seeks to dismantle the ruling state and replace it with another. The idea of Khizesh as Intifada finally breaks that vicious cycle.

I now believe that living with the truth of tyranny is actually better than living with the lie of democracy—for the simple fact that the long tiresome experiment with democracy resulted in and ended with Trump and all his European, Asian, African, and Latin American counterparts. In our part of the world, Israel, a barefaced barbarity of European colonialism built on the broken but defiant backs of Palestinians, considers itself "the only democracy in the Middle East." Paradoxically, they are right. For if that ugly truth of European colonialism is "democracy," no decent human being anywhere else in the world would wish to have anything to do with that lie.

Israel is the prototype of a garrison state that is the blueprint for all other illegitimate states that have long lost their claim to democratic representation. Israel is a European settler colonial state without a legitimate nation ruling over a Palestinian nation without a state. Like all other human beings, Jews belong to whatever nation of which they are citizens—in Europe, Americas, Palestine, or anywhere else. It is a profound act of Jewish hatred to assume all Jews must live in a European settler colony with a Masada complex. The systematic slaughter of Palestinians in Gaza in the aftermath of October 7, 2023, was the latest salvo in the incremental genocide of a nation in the cruel hands of European colonial savagery that is at the root of American imperial designs for the region and the world.

Trapped inside their myopic and cliché politics, the Iranian left, alas, failed to understand October 7 and its aftermath that is targeting the entire population, 2.3 million inhabitants, of Gaza. They have divided the Iranian reaction to the event into three categories: the reactionary right that sided with Israel; the reactionary Islamists who sided with Hamas; and the progressive socialists who denounced both Zionists and reactionary Islamists—and they thought they were really clever and progressive in doing so. But in doing so they exposed their deep-rooted ignorance of the Palestinian cause and their own equally recalcitrant Islamophobia. The categorization these Iranian leftists offered is the clear indication of a terrible misreading of the Palestinian national liberation movement. At the heart of Palestinian resistance to the Israeli settler colony remains a local, regional, and global Intifada (Khizesh). Any and all other aspirations to national liberation from domestic tyranny or globalized conditions of coloniality (in Iran or anywhere else) can claim a shred of legitimacy only to the degree that their Khizesh approximates an Intifada.

The German "left," meanwhile, was even more morally vacuous in actively siding with Israel and even with the United States.

According to one UK-based news outlet, "a movement rooted in radical left opposition to the German state became a vehicle for claiming all Palestine solidarity is antisemitic."[13] The report further explains:

> At a demonstration in the east German city of Leipzig in early November, the blue and white of the Israeli flag and the red and black flag of the antifa (anti-fascist) movement were seen flying together. Chants approved by the protest's organizers included "no God, no state, no caliphate" but also "fight for Zionism." A third chant identified this incongruous rally: "Nie wieder Deutschland"—never again Germany.

Echoing the same Islamophobic, racist, and genocidal urges, the leading German philosopher Jürgen Habermas was seen in this obscene spectacle of unconditional support for the Israeli genocide of Palestinians. The guilt that German intellectuals and so-called leftists may feel for what their parental generation did to Jews during the Holocaust has degenerated into supporting the Israeli genocide of Palestinians. By siding with Israel, Habermas in effect became the rightful descendant of Martin Heidegger and his infamous membership in the Nazi Party. With the abject horror of genocide in the aftermath of October 7, our very understanding of social uprisings and a quest for a democratic future has assumed a deeply troubled twist—if Israel is the crowning achievement of Western democracy, and if the sustained course of a remorseless genocide of Palestinians was endorsed and embraced by leading German and European critical thinkers, then the fate of humanity is to be found somewhere at the furthest remove from anything "European."

The struggle of nations for self-determination ought to no longer be under the self-defeating delusion of a struggle for democracy. We are liberated, body and soul, from that colonial lie and can preempt our political consciousness from being implicated in the so-called political process, or geared toward the formation of the next tyrannical state. Iran's successive attempts at democracy have vaccinated it against both the prospect and therefore the pipe dream of democracy. Democracy is not to be desired but forfeited. These young people in the streets of Tehran screaming "Death to the Dictator" are nihilist, perhaps even anarchist, suspicious of any and all state formations. Alexis de Tocqueville's observation in his *Democracy in America* (1835–1840) rings true now more than ever:

> Under the absolute government of one man, despotism, to reach the soul, crudely struck the body; and the soul, escaping from these blows, rose gloriously above it; but in democratic republics, tyranny does not proceed in this way; it leaves the body alone and goes right to the soul. The master no longer says: You will think like me or die; he says: You are free not to think as I do; your life, your goods, everything remains with you; but from this day on you are a stranger among us. You will keep your privileges as a citizen, but they will become useless to you.[14]

I can testify to the truth of that fact as a person born and raised in the Pahlavi tyranny who forever left his homeland and never returned to the Islamist theocracy that succeeded it. Then as an immigrant in the United States who never had the illusion that its white supremacist democracy that fully supported a Jewish supremacist garrison state in Palestine was ever applicable to me or to any other disenfranchised native or immigrant. The talk of martial law in the United States during the last few weeks of Trump's presidency (2017–2021) was no feeble matter. With only a month remaining until the end of his presidency, Trump was convinced—and millions of Americans were equally convinced with him—that the US presidential election was a fraud, that he had actually won but the election was rigged. As people were getting ready to celebrate their Christmas under the COVID-19 lockdown in the United States and elsewhere, Michael Flynn, Trump's pardoned former national security adviser, had already suggested the martial law plan on Newsmax and was invited to the White House to discuss further details.[15] "Democracy" was always a trap set by white people to keep colored people under control, and when we have laid a claim on that democracy, millions of these white people refused to pretend it was a legitimate project. On the colonial edges of capitalist modernity, this fact has always been doubly true. Democracy was never meant for colonized people. It was a trap. The fall 2022 uprising in Iran openly declared and announced it for the whole world to see. Predicated on that fact, a total revolution that will replace this delusional claim on democracy with yet another one—promised by Reza Pahlavi or Maryam Rajavi—is foolhardy. Khizesh-e Zhina as Intifada has finally brought the truth of that historical experience to full consciousness.

There are far more subversive elements to this uprising if we are to think of it in these terms—all rooted in this fateful exposure of the mirage of democracy. The revolt against mandatory veiling, for example, is the revolt against sectarian identity politics of "Islam and the West"—or the colonial divide between "Islam and Secularism"—for this revolt is not against Islam or for secularism; the whole false, colonially conditioned binary has finally collapsed, and as such the implications of this uprising are global. My contention therefore hovers around the question of women leading this uprising, but think it not accidental or an excuse for the uprising at large, for it is definitive to this moment through its intersectionality. It in fact questions the identity politics played by a generation of anthropologists who could not see a Muslim woman for anything but a veiled (Muslim) woman, signaled by a scarf, forced or voluntary—in opposition to the "secular West," which in effect had determined the dominant discourse. This debilitating binary I finally broke down in my recent book *The End of Two Illusions* (2022), thus seeking to restore worldly complexity to Muslim (Iranian) women and men alike, thus reasserting their historical agency, breaking them loose from generations of false binary consciousness.[16] Defiance against mandatory veiling is defiance against the bodily codification of state power that is scripted not just in the colonial heritage but in the postcolonial project of state-building.

The events of 2022 to 2023 in Iran occurred in the aftermath of various forces coming together to form the amorphous shape of a "total state" sustained via "pure violence" perpetrated on vulnerable civilians in the Levant and broader region: whether by the United States and NATO forces in Iraq or Libya, or by the Islamic State of Iraq and the Levant (ISIL) in Istanbul, Baghdad, Medina, Nice, or San Bernardino. ISIL is not an Islamic product. It is a product of colonial modernity in Muslim lands. ISIL is the return of the barely repressed origin of all states, for which all innocent civilians have become what the Italian philosopher Giorgio Agamben has aptly called "homo sacer" (the accursed person, the bare life). Unable to protect their citizens—as ISIL showed—all states it targets effectively lose their basis of legitimacy and become, like ISIL, a state without a nation supporting them. ISIL targeted the hyphen holding together the very idea of a "nation-state." Both the vicious ISIL and all its powerful nemeses fight their battles on the increasingly weakened, vulnerable, frightened, naked, exposed, dispensable, digitized, atomized bodies of innocent civilians. ISIL is the very definition of the state on steroids. With every attack by ISIL—or any other Islamist gang—against defenseless citizens of a sovereign state, that state becomes increasingly more like ISIL: absolutist, militaristic, opting for undemocratic measures to curtail civil liberties. The attempted military coup and countercoup in Turkey in 2016 are the most potent examples of relentless ISIL attacks pushing the states it targets toward militaristic measures. So is the rise of the proto-fascist Trump and pro–mass surveillance Hillary Clinton in the United States, or the rising popularity of xenophobic and Islamophobic political parties in Europe. The most symbolic version of it is the UK's Brexit vote—a potent combination of xenophobia and racism.

The end of the myth of the postcolonial state means the implosion of all the self-declared models of democracy in "the West," where we in the postcolonial world have been the wrong prototype to look up to. Trump's resounding defeat in the 2020 presidential election by some seven million popular votes and a decisive margin of Electoral College votes did not convince a massive portion of Americans that this election was not rigged.[17] The entire Republican Party was implicated in the attempted electoral coup that resulted in the storming of the Capitol on January 6, 2021, to prevent the peaceful transfer of power. Trump attempted to use major government institutions, all the way up to the Supreme Court, to facilitate this electoral coup. Millions of Americans remain convinced the election was rigged. These are adult, voting, and perfectly sane people. No amount of liberal chest-beating and hand-wringing is going to change that a rank charlatan, racist, misogynist, xenophobic white supremacist reached the highest office of the land and that even after four years of documented criminal behavior, he still had millions upon millions of supporters who remained loyal to him. It is believed that one out of three Americans, 77 percent of the Republicans, think the election was rigged. The underlying force of these numbers is the pandemic of conspiracy theories that effectively defines a politically powerful segment of the American electorate. Meanwhile, armed gangs were ready to storm other federal and state buildings around the country and were sending death threats to officials who had approved Trump's defeat. The violent conspiracy theories extend into public health issues, as a result of which the death toll among the poor and vulnerable populations in the United States is larger than anywhere else in the world. Add to that the fact that millions of Americans do not believe there is any climate calamity threatening earth. American democracy, in short, is an existential threat to the world at large, not an inspiration to it. Generations of postcolonial people grew up thinking of the United States and Europe as the model of liberal democracy. That delusion is fortunately now over. The Iranian uprising of 2022 to 2023 is the first post-democratic evidence of it. The case I make here against the cruel mirage of democracy, rooted in our collective historical experiences, is a cause for celebration and an occasion to think through successions of uprisings in our homelands, a crescendo of Khizeshes and Intifadas, as the modus operandi of our liberated political stance.

THE POSTHUMAN PERSON LEADING
A POST-DEMOCRATIC REVOLT

This post-democratic Zhina uprising recasts the thrust of Intifada as Khizesh into a theoretical cornerstone of reading it as an event. It is also necessary to grapple with and understand the posthuman persona that has, over at least the last quarter of a century, radically altered our perception of human agency presumed at the forefront of any revolutionary mobilization or collective behavior. At least since the events of 9/11 and the rise of suicidal violence, I have been preoccupied with the specifics of the posthuman body.[18] Rosi Braidotti has been a leading critical philosopher in this field, questioning our classical conception of humanism and social sciences. When Europeans began asserting that "man is the measure of all things" they never paused to wonder what exactly they meant by "man"—for they always assumed a white, heterosexual, male European person was that "man." Generations of feminist scholars and scholars of race, gender, sexuality, and colonialism have seriously advanced our received masculinist reading of that European "man." But today something even more basic is challenging the proposition of our humanity. The white heterosexual conquering the earth as the agent at the heart of what had congratulated itself as "Western humanism" is no longer. In her extensive body of work, Braidotti details the paradoxes of posthuman intelligence, reaching for a convergence of digital afterlife, the genetically modified food we now consume, the artificial intelligence that is threatening the working class, all coming together to dismantle the way we have understood human agency, or even the unity of the posthuman being.

Braidotti asks, Who or what exactly is a human being anyway? As she rightly puts it:

This Eurocentric paradigm implies the dialectics of self and other, and the binary logic of identity and otherness as, respectively, the motor for and the cultural logic of universal Humanism. Central to this universalistic posture and its binary logic is the notion of "difference" as pejoration. Subjectivity is equated with consciousness, universal rationality, and self-regulating ethical behavior, whereas Otherness is defined as its negative and specular counterpart.[19]

In what language, therefore, can we talk of a people's uprising against tyranny to make it universally understood if and when those people are deuniversalized, particularized, ethnicized, and subjected to colonial (anthropological) observations? Generations of critical thinking are behind dismantling Europocentric humanism. We on the (post)colonial edges of the world have faced up to and dismantled this moment: "In so far as difference spells inferiority, it acquires both essentialist and lethal connotations for people who get branded as 'other.' These are the sexualized, racialized, and naturalized others who are reduced to the less-than-human status of disposable bodies." In and of itself these are belated confessions in the field. But they are still very much welcomed. "We are all humans," Braidotti reminds us, "but some of us are just more mortal than others. Because their history in Europe and elsewhere has been one of lethal exclusions and fatal disqualifications, these 'others' raise issues of power and exclusion."[20] These meditations on posthuman humanism raise the question of specifying the postcolonial subject standing behind the utterance of revolt against tyranny. If the Zhina uprising is not to be yet another gestation of "third-world revolution" against "Oriental despotism," it will have to be mapped out in terms at home with these posthuman conditions. Tyranny dehumanizes our humanity. The Zhina uprising is a moment of reasserting a people's humanity in an irreversibly posthuman world. With a decidedly radical twist, Braidotti moves toward a whole different mode of reading our transformed humanity:

> For me there is a necessary link between critical posthumanism and the move beyond anthropocentrism. I refer to this move as expanding the notion of Life toward the nonhuman or zoe. This results in radical posthumanism as a position that transposes hybridity, nomadism, diasporas and creolization processes into means of re-grounding claims to subjectivity, connections and community among subjects of the human and the nonhuman kind.[21]

Definitive to that hybridity beyond anthropomorphism is the public persona of people, in or out of their homeland, with their own names or with a pseudonym, on social media. That rampant phenomenon, too, is an aspect of a posthuman (nonhuman) person. A politically significant proportion of Iranians, as many other people, are on social media screaming against tyranny and articulating a free and liberated world they wish to see in their lifetimes. Social media has had a serious presence and significance in most recent uprisings. This might be seen as a healthy indicator of a society that the internet activists represent as on the verge of a political upheaval. But these screams, nasty and brutish at times, are also against their own kind, against other Iranians they hate and despise for nonexistent and unreal reasons. Slander, rumor, conspiracy theories, obscenities, and threats of violence are at a level impossible to imagine before what social media has made possible. Social media has given birth to a particularly brutish persona, especially among the diasporic communities that are overcompensating for the freedom of expression they have lacked with vile and violent public behavior under the guise of the anonymity they have created for themselves. Critical posthumanism that seeks to go beyond anthropomorphism at the point of *zoe* must come to terms with the sheer barbarism of social media. This barbarism is not temporary or caused by moments of acute anxieties of a revolt. It is real, it is permanent, and it is here to stay. The fictive character of a posthuman persona leading a post-democratic uprising is the prelude to artificial intelligence and internet bots leading revolutions. As the world worries about AI taking over human jobs, I am convinced that the first generation of those robots are right in front of us in the shape of a platoon of Pahlavi monarchists spamming their presumed nemeses on social media, spewing monarchist propaganda and disinformation, violently rewriting the history of the Pahlavi monarchy. And they are met and raised by similar internet bots and bogs the Islamic Republic has generated to protect itself. No assessment of a post-democratic uprising can remain ignorant of such posthuman revolutionary bots.

THE HOUSE OF THE IDRISIS

It is therefore in the enduring works of film, fiction, drama, and poetry where literary characters stage a different dramatic posthumanism that we may go back to revisit as literary subjects, and where the fears and aspirations of their presence in any post-democratic uprising on the premise of a predemocratic history still resonates. As a crucial example, Ghazaleh Alizadeh's signature novel, *The House of the Idrisis* (1991), became even more tragically iconic following her suicide on May 12, 1996.[22] The story is set in the early twentieth century in a fictional city called Eshq-abad that may or may not

be Ashgabat, the capital city of the Republic of Turkmenistan. The
Idrisis' house is under the towering shadow of its matriarch, the aris-
tocratic Mrs. Idrisi, surrounded by her daughter Laqa, her grandson
Vahab, and their servant Yavar. A revolution that may or may not be
that of 1977 to 1979 in Iran takes place, and a gang of revolutionaries
invades and occupies the ancient and venerable house with its inhabitants as effective hostages. The revolutionaries are a mixed bag of
wide-eyed idealists and haphazard ruffians, neither vilified nor val-
orized, led by an aggressive woman named Shokat. The revolution
goes sour; a revolution within the revolution takes place and a group
of rebels moves to the surrounding mountains. Counterrevolution-
aries become revolutionaries of their own with a deeper mythic force
informing their politics.

In his review of the novel, Mohammad Mokhtari, a leading literary critic of his time who is widely believed to have been murdered
by the security forces of the Islamic Republic, believes the opening
sentence of the novel is an homage to Tolstoy's *Anna Karenina*.[23]
Mokhtari also notes that the omniscient narrator speaks through
these four characters, which we may take even further to suggest
that the four characters are all shades of the same persona. The same
is true with the timing, which Mokhtari also divides into three different kinds of pasts.[24] This divides the story into four generations,
which gives the novel a cross-like (*salibi*) structure. Based on this
and other critical readings of the novel, we might suggest what happens in this novel is the active literary transformation of a radical
revolution that toppled a monarchy, miserably failed to restore any
democratic hope, and degenerated into an Islamic theocracy. These
historical facts are dissolved into the raw material for a far more
important metamorphosis of the revolutionary urge into literary
transmutation of facts. Through a poetic diction unmatched in her

generation, Alizadeh turned a terrifying political upheaval into a literary meditation on more enduring but subterranean changes. The book itself became the sublimation of the revolution it depicted and raised it to a literary event. For this reason, we might also consider it an Iranian version of Gabriel García Márquez's *One Hundred Years of Solitude* (1967), the story of seven generations of the Buendía family in the town of Macondo, which here becomes four generations of the Idrisi family in the city of Eshq-abad. The same way that *One Hundred Years of Solitude* was a literary rendition of Colombian, and by extension Latin American, history, the *House of the Idrisis* might also be considered a literary rendition not just of the Iranian Revolution but of the entirety of Iranian history.

If we abandon the false anxiety of radical revolutions that will dismantle tyranny for good and inaugurate democracy and instead see the world in a succession of Intifadas and Khizeshes, through the metonymic power of the literary world we become aware of far more enduring posthuman prospects, where the real (invisible) revolutions are plowing the fertile ground of the unfolding history. These uprisings are not geared toward the dismantling of one political regime in anticipation of establishing the next. They are sowing the seeds of a radically different persona at the roots of our posthuman evidence in a post-democratic hope for liberation. The principal objective of such uprisings is to discredit the false claims of legitimacy of not just this state but any other state to come.

FIVE

DO IRANIAN WOMEN NEED SAVING?

What happened in 2022 was a kind of coalition among the subalterns that gathered momentum around a noneconomic factor with the centrality of women and of being marginalized. The issues of women and tyranny against women created a women's uprising in which both the young people in [the more affluent Tehran neighborhoods of] Sa'adat-abad and Tehran Pars could see themselves as did the Kurds and the Baluch. In other words, the centrality of injustice against women in this uprising made a kind of coalition possible that was otherwise impossible to imagine before.

—**Aghil Daghagheleh** (March 2023)

In a timely essay on the Zhina uprising, Noushin Ahmadi Khorasani, a leading Iranian feminist and women's rights activist, raised the potent question: "What are the reasons that the gray layer did not join the 'Zan, Zendegi, Azadi' uprising?"[1] "The gray layer" (*Qeshr-e Khakestari*) is a common phrase applied to those parts of Iranian society at large that may have had passive sympathy for the uprising but did not actively join it. They are neither black (supporters of the regime) nor white (those who wish it overthrown)—and therefore they are gray. As one of the most widely published, active, and recognized women's rights activists, Khorasani is in a position to raise these kinds of larger political issues, for no one doubts her primary preoccupation with the status of women and their freedom of choice to wear or not to wear the hijab.

Ahmadi Khorasani writes that in 2017, when Vida Movahed, a young women's rights activist, stood in the middle of a busy Tehran street and took off her scarf and hung it on a stick in protest of mandatory veiling, scarce anyone thought it a revolutionary moment. But the selfsame acts in 2022 were universally considered a turning point in the prolonged history of successive uprisings against the Islamist regime. Khorasani wonders why. What has happened in the course of these five years? In 2017, there was much hope and enthusiasm about Vida Movahed's heroic act, but it remained at a level of a bold gesture by an activist who was fed up by the mandatory hijab and publicly took the violent authorities to task. Bold and subversive as the act was, it did not trigger any major event. Khorasani considers how the parental generation of the young Iranians has always tried to prevent their children from trusting any radical change, for they had themselves been bitten by the same enthusiasm and severely punished by the state. The parental middle class was doing its best to create a "Golkhaneh" (greenhouse) at home for their children, she believes, and to send their children abroad when and if they could afford it. That kind of thinking evidently worked for the middle class particularly well between 2017 and 2022, but not anymore. Khorasani now believes that the worsening economic conditions are a key factor in explaining the current uprising, when the parental generation voted for President Hassan Rouhani (in office from 2013 to 2021), thinking the nuclear deal with the United States would work out and that the economic crisis would be at least partially resolved. But when Donald Trump came to power and dismantled the deal in May 2018, and the ruling radical reactionaries joined Trump in that disruptive act, that hope was smashed. The worsening global economy under the COVID-19 lockdown in 2020 to 2021 was also a key factor that helped eliminate that middle-class buffer zone between the ruling state and the youthful uprising.

In a way, as Ahmadi Khorasani understands it, the parental middle class was a key element in sustaining the ruling regime in power for its own economic interests. But it had ultimately failed, and the dismantling of the nuclear deal by Trump, and the subsequent election of the corrupt and inept Ebrahim Raisi to office in August 2021, was the death knell of the middle class's aspirations. Between the Green Movement (2009 to 2010) and the Zhina uprising of 2022, there were few other revolts by the poorer classes, but this current movement brought the middle and the lower classes, the liberal and radical ideas, together and also revealed a generational gap. The opposition to mandatory veiling, Khorasani thinks, had created divisions along at least three lines: generational, class, and religious affinity. The revolt against mandatory veiling, she believes, is at the expense of a more radical uprising to topple the regime. Moreover, she says the emphasis on mandatory veiling had prevented those who had voluntarily opted to veil from joining the uprising.

MUSLIM WOMEN, ISLAM, REVOLT

The significance of this timely essay by Noushin Ahmadi Khorasani is manifold, but perhaps most important is the fact that a leading Iranian feminist has a thoroughly economic reading of the Zhina uprising, to the point that she submits the all-too-important issue of mandatory veiling to more cogent economic factors. The parental middle-class generation obviously seeks to protect its children from the vicious violence of the ruling state and thus has acted to the best of its abilities as a buffer between state violence and its children. But a global pandemic, a violent US president beholden to Zionist forces, and the equally reactionary forces inside Iran have exacerbated economic conditions, and these children have no more reasons or hope left not to pour into streets. There are a few issues with Khorasani's analysis to be sure. If the parents have run out of economic wherewithal to protect their children, then they must join them in the streets, but based on this analysis they did not. Why? The other issue is that in her haste to underline the economic factors, all cogent, she dismisses the mandatory veiling issue and discounts its symbolic significance in opposing and seeking to end the ruling Islamist regime.

As evident in Ahmadi Khorasani's essay and many other insights like it, central to the Women, Life, Freedom uprising of 2022 in Iran is the issue of women and their social status and economic well-being—and that is not a mere slogan. It is definitive to the movement as it marks the political aspirations, social concerns, and economic predicament of Iranian women. But how do we locate the issue of women's status in Iran within the larger context of regional and global politics? For this uprising has to be read in that larger context to assume its innate historic significance.

Otherwise, the cartoonish monarchists from California are hard at work changing the nature and disposition of this uprising as a belated and outdated cause for Pahlavi royalists.

About a decade ago the distinguished anthropologist Lila Abu-Lughod published a book in which she asked the provocative question, *Do Muslim Women Need Saving?*[2] Abu-Lughod rightly understood the systematic abuse of Muslim women's issues in the major European and US media and human rights venues as a form of ideological subterfuge to demonize countries like Afghanistan, Iraq, or Iran to prepare public opinion for military attacks. Abu-Lughod rightly targets human rights organizations and the corporate media for turning the fate of Muslim women into an ideological cornerstone of military strikes and subservient state-building projects on the failed models of Afghanistan and Iraq. She equally persuasively demonstrates how issues of gender apartheid and the violation of women's rights are endemic to the global condition that implicates secular "Western" democracies. As a result, the aggressive demonization of Islam is more an ideological subterfuge for imperial projects rather than a genuine care for the well-being of Muslim women.

In her 2002 *American Anthropologist* essay of the same title (later expanded into the previously mentioned book), Abu-Lughod linked her rhetorical question to "the ethics of the current 'War on Terror,' asking whether anthropology, the discipline devoted to understanding and dealing with cultural difference, can provide us with critical purchase on the justification made for American intervention in Afghanistan in terms of liberating, or saving, Afghan women."[3] All may not agree that anthropology, a discipline that was created and has remained at the service of European colonialism, was ever in the business of "understanding cultural difference" except in a way that would serve those very European colonial interests.[4] Nor do we need to invoke the discipline of anthropology—and its poverty of "critical purchase"—or any other colonially mitigated discipline to realize that abusing the status of women in the course of the so-called war on terror was a treacherous ideological ruse and had no base in any "ethics" except the brute politics of imperial domination of the globe. Be that as it may, the point of Abu-Lughod about the abuse of women's status remains solid—entirely independent of the deeply compromised discipline of anthropology.

Today we can echo Abu-Lughod's question in a slightly modified way and ask if Iranian women—the overwhelming majority of them Muslim, in one way or another—leading a national uprising in their homeland, need to be saved from their own culture. Iranian women and girls in their tens of thousands all across their homeland poured into streets burning their scarves and protesting mandatory veiling. That potent fact, that defiant rebellion against a pernicious Islamic clerical patriarchy, is also their culture. So, obviously, they need not be liberated by US Marines while their fathers and husbands and brothers are tortured and abused in a prison like Guantánamo. But at the same time, how are we to consider Iranian women and girls burning their scarves? Is that not Islamophobic? Would that not be documented by human rights organizations? Might Hillary Clinton not jump on the bandwagon and speak on their behalf? Would those gestures not discredit these Iranian women's uprisings?

The issue overrides any disciplinary preoccupation with anthropology, sociology, political science, or any other such discipline that has been compromised by being quintessentially Eurocentric in its critical imagination. The more basic question remains: How does this protest against veiling bear on the questions of gender, religion, and above all the bugbear of "modernity"? The ruling regime in Iran calls itself an Islamic republic—and no one is in a position to say the leading Shi'i authorities who run the state are not Muslims, and Islam is something else. Islam might very well be quite a number of other things. But this Islamic republic is also Islamic—and millions of Iranian women and girls are revolting against its tyrannical, draconian, outdated, violent, and patriarchal regime. Are these Iranian women not Muslim? How are we to understand their revolt against an *Islamic* republic? No doubt, the United States, Israel, and Saudi Arabia (another major Muslim country) wish to abuse the Women, Life, Freedom uprising in Iran to their benefit and to change the belligerent Islamist regime to their own benefit. But do any of these facts discredit Iranian women as Muslim women rising up against this Islamic republic? Do Muslim women in Iran and Afghanistan owe a pledge of allegiance to the two blatantly Islamic regimes that brutally rule over them? The answer, of course, is no—pure and simple. But the answer also creates an epistemic twist at the heart of Abu-Lughod's argument and by extension the whole discipline of anthropology she so well represents: Can Muslim women save themselves from a vicious Islamic republic without any aid from "the West"?

SOME FACTS ON THE GROUND

Let us look at some of the facts on the ground: "Iranian security forces are targeting women at antiregime protests with shotgun fire to their faces, breasts and genitals, according to interviews with medics across the country."⁵ This is according to professional journalists working at the *Guardian*. For those of us who have been following Persian sources from inside and outside the country, this ghastly fact was no news. "Doctors and nurses—treating demonstrators in secret to avoid arrest—said they first observed the practice after noticing that women often arrived with different wounds to men, who more commonly had shotgun pellets in their legs, buttocks and backs."⁶ Women who were burning their mandatory scarves in protest were decidedly targeted in their faces (especially their eyes) and genitalia by the security forces of one solidly and unquestionably Islamic republic.

No amount of liberal meandering and anthropological dilly-dallying about "the Western press" could compromise that fact. The reports of human rights organizations like Amnesty International corroborate such facts: "Iran: Authorities Covering Up Their Crimes of Child Killings by Coercing Families into Silence."⁷ "The Iranian authorities' arbitrary arrest, intimidation and harassment of relatives of children, unlawfully gunned down or beaten to death by security forces in connection with protests, exposes their inconceivable cruelty and sinister attempt to cover up their crimes,"⁸ reports Amnesty International. Just to state the obvious: the ruling apparatus of the Islamic Republic in Iran knowingly targets women and girls for having dared to defy mandatory veiling and to express their wish to choose whether to wear the so-called hijab.

Let us now revisit the question: Do Muslim women need saving? And in this particular case do Iranian women need saving from a depraved Islamic republic? The answer is most definitely yes. But *they* are doing their own saving—not the US Marines or NATO bombs and "humanitarian interventions." They are revolting against an Islamist regime, and they are not part of US-Israel propaganda to demonize Islam. The revolt against mandatory veiling is not against veiling but against the more fundamental power of toxic patriarchal masculinity that abuses veiling as an insignia of violence against women's bodies and their freedom to choose. What the Zan, Zendegi, Azadi uprising indicates is that Iranian women, precisely as Muslim women, or even if they choose not to so identify themselves, are irreducible to their being Muslims based on assumptions of reactionary or liberal ideologies outside their own historical spheres. The partition of women between rich and poor, educated and uneducated, secular and religious, nativist or "Westernized" have all completely lost their false currencies here. The lived experiences of Iranian women have given birth to a different take on intersectionality—not something to be strived for but something deeply rooted in their own history. This particular historical moment also raises the inadequacy of the term "secular" in understanding the lived experience of a Muslim population defying mandatory veiling. Iranian women are not being "secular" when rejecting mandatory veiling imposed on them against their will. They are being entirely true to the pluralistic experiences of their history, which includes being Muslim and includes exposure to colonial modernity but is not reducible to either of them. The term "secular" as a subterfuge for colonial modernity is woefully inadequate and has no legitimate "genealogy" within this particular society of Muslim citizens.

Yes, the majority of these women demonstrating in Iran against mandatory veiling are Muslim, but they are much more than the terms "Muslim" or "Islam" can command or define for them in the colonial context of "Islam and the West" or a fortiori the colonial legacy of the discipline of anthropology. Their historical and active awareness of their non-Islamic (not anti-Islamic) heritage is equally important. Being Iranian, or Egyptian, or Indian can certainly include being a Muslim but is not exhausted by it. The choice is not between being Muslim and being "secular" (for which there is no word or "genealogy" in Persian, Arabic, Turkish, or Urdu). The choice is between being exclusively Muslim, as defined by "the West," and nothing else, and being openly Iranian and embracing the totality of their historical heritage. This has far-reaching implications for the entire women's rights movement in the region. Ever since the establishment of Pakistan and Israel as Islamic and Jewish states, their delusionary sectarian identities have replaced the pluralistic fact of people's lived experiences. A Jewish woman is not just Jewish (as defined by Zionism) and with the same token a Muslim woman is not just Muslim (as defined by Islamism)—especially the way the terms have been decided for them in a false binary between "religious and secular" in a colonial context over which they had little to no control.

When the Green Movement started back in 2009, I suggested that it was the restoration of the Iranian cosmopolitan culture—and now these terms are even stronger.[9] We need a new paradigm that the existing sentiments of major critical thinkers who have fallen victim to the "Islam and the West" binary have left unexamined in their thinking.[10] Opposing imperial interventions and colonial domination of the world should not translate into turning a blind eye to the terror of religious or secular fanaticism on the home front. This new post-Western paradigm should not abandon the crucial critique of colonialism and Orientalism. Quite the contrary, it will expand it—but it will not fixate on a delusional enemy and give it metaphysical power. We are not to abandon the critique of the tyranny of the domestic dictator just because they pretend they are fighting the West or its favorite settler colony Israel. Much of the critical apparatus crafted by leading scholars of the field is predicated on an identity politics that was crafted within the false binary of "Islam and the West" as the most potent legacy of colonial modernity, where women were cast into a singular site of contestation against the West that had remained consistent since Fanon's deeply flawed reading of veiling in Algeria.[11] The question is not veiling or unveiling. The question is a matter of agency—which is precisely the point of the current uprising, where the revolt is not against voluntary but against mandatory veiling.

The genealogy of my own thinking about the matter is important here: At the time of my reading the Arab Spring uprisings of 2010s, I insisted that this is the end of the myth of the postcolonial state—and at the time of publishing *The Emperor Is Naked: The Inevitable Demise of the Nation-State* (2020), I argued that the postcolonial state had been stripped of any and all legitimacy.[12] By the time I wrote *The End of Two Illusions: Islam after the West* (2022), I was completely liberated from any entrapment of reading Islam or Muslims within the boundaries that this fiction of the West had created for them. The Zhina uprising in Iran is the first post-Western uprising where the illusion of "the West" is no longer the measure of anything and by the same token the "Islam" that this "West" had crafted has ceased to exist. The Islamist thuggeries of the ruling regime in Iran are the dead end of that colonially manufactured Islam. Muslims are not bound by what European Orientalists or American anthropologists have made of their ancestral faith. It is a truism that Iranian women don't need saving but not in the sense that the liberal critique of Islamophobia means Muslim women don't need saving. This time around, their liberation is not from Islam as such but from the colonially constituted Islam in which academic politics has been trapped. Much of the critical scholarship produced by liberal feminists in academia against Islamophobia and in defense of Muslim women is itself trapped within the binary of Islam and the West, in effect contributing to that false and falsifying binary, where the insignia of a Muslim woman is reduced to her choice of wearing the hijab rather than choosing not to wear it.

The powerful feminist uprising in Iran, named after its first victim, Mahsa Zhina Amini, liberates Muslim women across the Muslim world from this false fetishization of veiling as the singular definition of being Muslim, a forced metaphor imposed on Muslim women by being trapped inside a false binary of Islam and the West. Dismantle that false binary and Muslim women are free to wear or not to wear the hijab based on their choice. Muslim women as Muslim women must be granted the freedom to choose the public appearance with which they wish to be part of the larger world. This freedom of choice, the harbinger of a post-Islamism liberation theology—the contours of which I have already outlined in some detail[13]—is far superior to the forced metaphor of Muslim women wearing the hijab in order to prove their bodies are immune from "Western" influence. With the Zan, Zendegi, Azadi uprising in Iran, the entire generation of scholarship that argued that Muslim women are happy with their hijab, so don't try to liberate them, will have to be radically reconsidered. Some Muslim women are happy and proud of their hijabs; others are not and are risking their lives publicly burning them and dancing around that fire. The mullahs in Qom and anthropologists around the world must come to terms with that fact.

The larger historical context of the Zhina uprising is also exceedingly important to keep in mind. Over the last two centuries alone, Iranian women have been fighting for their rights against the backdrop of the larger social and economic maladies of their homeland. From the middle of the nineteenth century onward, they have fought against the two monarchic dynasties of the Qajars and the Pahlavis and now an Islamic republic.[14] That longevity gives their current revolt against a vicious theocracy a whole different timbre and tonality. They are revolting against this Islamic republic not because it is Islamic but because it is a tyranny perpetrated in specifically Islamic terms. Yes, the majority of these Iranian women were born and raised as Shi'i Muslims, but that is not all that they are. They are also Iranian, which has a whole different set of connotations, not all of which are nationalistic in an ideological way. They come from poorer or more middle-class backgrounds, all of them searching for a decent life. They were not born to this life to be told violently to take off their veils by one monarchic thug like Reza Shah and then to put them back on by another Islamic thug like Ayatollah Khomeini.

WOMEN'S STATUS AND ISLAMIC LAW: A CUL-DE-SAC

As best represented by Abu-Lughod's study, much of the idea of "Muslim women" (and not just among anthropologists) is conceived and understood primarily in English (and French and other European languages) from outside the Muslim world and tends to disregard the divisions and pluralism of what it means to be a Muslim woman from the lived experiences of Muslim women in a rapidly changing world. The very term "Muslim countries" (or even "Muslim-majority countries") is to be radically questioned. Not all people in these societies are Muslims, much less in a single way. But also, the predominance of such understandings applies mostly bourgeois feminism to certain key countries like Egypt, Syria, or Sudan, while the rural and working-class women in places like Lorestan, Khuzestan, Khorasan, Azerbaijan, Baluchistan, or Kurdish areas of Iran, Iraq, Syria, and Turkey, are not part of the conversation at all. The idea of "Muslim women" is also heavily Arabized at the expense of the vast majority of Muslim women who are not Arabs, as Turks, Kurds, Iranians, and South Asians live in a different cultural pluralism. In the case of Iran in particular, the idea of Muslim women is a radically ideological project, introduced by the ruling Islamist regime against the equally ideological idea of the "modern women" the Pahlavi dynasty was promoting as part of their own state-building projects. The textured realities of large countries like Iran, from the rural to the urban and from the peripheral to central, are vastly different from both these ideological contestations. Since the violent imposition of mandatory veiling was and remains an ideological project, opposition to it has also assumed a radically militant and ideological posture. If society at large is left to its own devices, a far more diversified and multivariant shape will emerge, with women's presence in the labor force as the final determining factor. No, Muslim women do not need saving, but the phrase "Muslim women" itself needs saving from false generalizations.

Just a couple of years before Lila Abu-Lughod's crucial volume, the leading Iranian feminist scholar Ziba Mir-Hosseini (also an anthropologist) and her colleagues edited and published a volume featuring writings from prominent Muslim women's rights activists and legal scholars (both women and men), titled *Gender and Equality in Muslim Family Law* (2013).[15] Issues of gender equality in Egypt and Morocco receive special attention in this volume, as do more theoretical discussions by such leading legal scholars like the late Nasr Abu Zayd from Egypt and Mohsen Kadivar from Iran. In this volume, these scholars place the central issue of gender equality in historical context and maintain that only recently has this issue become pertinent. It is only in the twentieth century, they maintain, that Muslim legal scholars began addressing gender equality. This is against the legal background that historically men have been the privileged sex by the mandates of Islamic law. These scholars are of the firm conviction that any enduring and sustainable change in the status of Muslim women must come from within the Muslim tradition itself by engaging with the more progressive forces inside the Islamic legal field. The admirable commitment of these scholars to work within the outdated, reactionary, and irredeemably misogynistic foundations of the status of women in Islamic law gives them the added advantage to expose the impossible task of reforming "Islamic law," as it has been handed down to legal authorities, mostly men, in positions of power when it comes to the status of women in any shape or form. What their scholarship reveals, however, is that this progressive group of Muslim women and men is actively engaged within their own tradition to tackle the sacrosanct elements of Islamic gender inequality—to what effect, history has proved minuscule.

If we were to put the insights, dedicated activism, and detailed knowledge of Noushin Ahmadi Khorasani (writing mostly in Persian) and Ziba Mir-Hosseini (writing mostly in English) together, the crucial factor that defines the current status of Muslim women in their own homelands and in their own terms (in the context of which the Zhina uprising is taking place) is the fusion of social status and economic participation, which has brought Muslim women to the forefront of the labor force. These women need no saving by US Marines or NATO bombs—we do not need the discipline of anthropology to go out of its colonial way to tell us that. But they do need saving (and they do the saving) from the most reactionary forces at work in the very texture of Islamic law, weaponized by militant Islamist ideologies and regimes like those of Iran and Afghanistan. The issue is not Islamic law per se—which might be imagined in abstraction in the most liberal, reactionary, or progressive terms. The issue is which Muslim jurists are in charge, and which are on the run. In Iran, Ali Khamenei and Mesbah Yazdi, the most reactionary jurists of their time, decide the fate of Iranian women, not Mohsen Kadivar, who has run away to exile in the United States and can stipulate his liberal interpretation of Islamic law from a safe distance and in total abstract liberalism. It is quite telling that the two prominent legal scholars Mir-Hosseini and her colleagues feature in their edited volume, Nasr Abu Zayd and Mohsen Kadivar, were both exiled from their homeland because of their views. Abu Zayd returned from Europe to Egypt just before his death in July 2010. Kadivar to this day remains in exile and cannot set foot in Iran without risking immediate arrest. They could be as open-minded, liberal, or even radical in their abstract thoughts. But those thoughts, expressed in an edited volume in English, have very little to no effect in a country where militant clerics and their armed gangs are in total charge of the legal apparatus of the country, where they shoot women in their genitalia if they dare protest mandatory veiling.

The issue, again, is not Islamic law in and of itself—as it is understood today. The issue is the decoupling of Islamic law from its historical location in the context of other intellectual forces definitive to Islam before its fateful and calamitous encounter with European colonial modernity, particularly its dialogical disputations with rational theology, peripatetic philosophy, homocentric mysticism, and Adab. This dissection of Islamic intellectual history has happened under colonial duress, when militant Muslim ideologues, from Muhammad Abduh (1849–1905) to Ayatollah Khomeini (1902–1989), weaponized Islamic law as a potent ideology that served their militant Islamism and state-building projects. The ruling Islamist regime in Iran, the drug dealers in charge of the Taliban takeover of Afghanistan (thanks to US military adventurism), and the ISIL cannibals in Iraq and Syria are variations on that theme. Ideologies like those of Ali Shariati, Abdolkarim Soroush, Hasan Yousefi Eshkevari, or Mohsen Kadivar have done their best to recast Islamic law in a more cogent contemporary context in dialogue with "modernity." But it is not accidental that all of these figures who are still alive now live in exile from their homeland, having done their initial services to over-Islamize Iranian political consciousness only to be cast aside by the selfsame ruling Islamist regime, which has only one interest: self-preservation at any cost. Islamic law for the ruling state is today totally severed from its historic conversations and contestation with its theological, philosophical, and mystical rivals. It is just a totalitarian state ideology, with women as its primary victims.

Islamic legal discourse, recast as Islamic ideology, did have a modicum of dialogue with aspects of colonial modernity, such as socialism and nationalism, before the Islamist takeover in Iran, when figures like Ali Shariati, Mahmoud Taleqani, or Morteza Motahhari were conversant with their ideological nemeses. As a result, their own political prose spoke a dialogical language. That dialogical language has completely disappeared, dissolved into the totalizing and triumphalist discourse of the ruling regime. This discourse of vindictive Islamism is no longer salvageable. It must be dismantled. Future Muslims need and will eventually craft a post-Islamist liberation theology—and the laws that must emerge from the collective will of the Muslim public consciousness will be articulated on the premise of that public sphere in which Islam is present and integral but not dominant or definitive.

WOMEN AND THE CONDITION OF SUBALTERNITY

In understanding the inner dynamics of the Zhina uprising it is imperative we listen carefully to the critical voices, like those of Noushin Ahmadi Khorasani, which are deeply informed and come from inside Iran—and especially those who write in Persian, with Iranians as their evident and active interlocutors. One example of such a voice is of a young critical thinker, Aghil Daghagheleh, with his recent essay, "Foru-dasti va Lahzeh Enqelabi-ye Zhina" (Subalternity and the Revolutionary Moment of Zhina).[16] Daghagheleh is a doctoral candidate in sociology at Rutgers University, but given the tenor and facility of his Persian prose and the venues in which he publishes he remains deeply and closely conversant with his peers inside Iran.[17] The key contribution of this essay is its attempt to link the centrality of women in this uprising with other disenfranchised subaltern groups in the Iranian context. Daghagheleh rightly suggests that there has always been a chasm between social uprisings of the center and the economic protests of the periphery. Mostly impoverished provinces have primarily economic concerns, and the relatively better-off bourgeois preoccupations of the center have primarily social concerns. He does not put this in exclusive terms. But his argument is well-founded. When there is a water shortage in Khuzestan, for example, or economic destitution in Baluchistan, these issues scarce matter to people in Tehran. Daghagheleh believes these barriers between center and periphery were crossed over in the course of the Zhina uprising; the ethnicized minorities kept their political identities and yet joined the center and vice versa. His point is that the subaltern disposition of the women's movement resonates with the economic deprivations around the country. He defines the condition of subalternity carefully:

> Subalternity is when individuals or groups are prevented entry into social and economic structures, and they have no roles in political decision-making. They are just the object of political domination. They are invisible, and in a variety of ways have been omitted from many social settings. This invisibility and disregard are particularly evident regarding the people of Baluchistan and Kurdistan. We scarce see or hear from them. Occasionally we notice them in the midst of events, just like buried but still alive sparks from under this edifice of modernity.[18]

Young people in Tehran, especially young women, identify with this condition of subalternity, for they too have been made invisible from social and political sights. There are therefore "three circles," as Daghagheleh sees it, in this uprising: Tehran, Baluchistan, and Kurdistan, and they have now concurred and acted together.

What follows from the logic of Daghagheleh's argument (but is outside his arguments in this particular essay) is the even more invisible condition of the LGBTQ+ communities in Iran (as elsewhere). In this particular case, the invisibility of this repressed and brutalized community is so deep and dark that there is not even a proper name or acronym for them in Persian, and they invariably use the acronym LGBTQ+ or else Queer to identify themselves. The word "Digar-bash" has been coined to designate the condition of alterity among the community, but they still have an uphill battle to receive recognition or even acknowledgment.[19] This, to be sure, is a global malady not exclusive to Iran. I write these sentences from the heart-less heart of the United States, where the homophobic culture of fear and loathing is standard operation for the entire Republican political party. But in Iran, in particular, "discrimination and violence against sexual minorities," according to Human Rights Watch, is systematic and rampant.[20] According to a Human Rights Watch official cited in this report: "Members of sexual minorities in Iran are hounded on all sides . . . . The laws are stacked against them; the state openly discriminates against them; and they are vulnerable to harassment, abuse, and violence because their perpetrators feel they can target them with impunity." The report specifically pinpoints the officials of the Islamic Republic as engaging in such violent behavior:

> Iran's security forces, including police and forces of the hard-line paramilitary *basij*, rely upon discriminatory laws to harass, arrest, and detain individuals whom they sus-pect of being gay, Human Rights Watch found. The inci-dents often occur in parks and cafes, but Human Rights Watch also documented cases in which security forces raided homes and monitored internet sites for the purpose of detaining people they suspected of engaging in noncon-forming sexual conduct or gender expression.[21]

Still, widespread awareness of Digar-Bashan is a clear indica-tion that no kind of injustice is isolated from the rest. The central-ity of women in the Zhina uprising must not conceal the even more dire circumstances of the LGBTQ+ community. The Islamist the-ocracy that rules over them all has systematically degenerated into a garrison state on the model of Israel that it rhetorically targets, and all citizens of this misnomer of a republic, just like Palestinians in their own homeland, are equally vulnerable to its whims.

SIX

"CROWD IS UNTRUTH"

*There is a view of life which holds that where the crowd
is, the truth is also, that it is a need in truth itself, that
it must have the crowd on its side. There is another view
of life; which holds that wherever the crowd is, there is
untruth, so that, for a moment to carry the matter out to
its furthest conclusion, even if every individual possessed
the truth in private, yet if they came together into a crowd
(so that "the crowd" received any decisive, voting, noisy,
audible importance), untruth would at once be let in.*

—**Søren Kierkegaard** (1847)

"Iran is inside me," she says. "I am there every single day through
my social media." The person who said these words said them while
in New York. How could she be in Iran every day? Who is she? She
is Masih Alinejad, or, more accurately, Masoumeh Alinejad-Ghomikolayi, who has made her name more palatable to her American
promoters. She is the Iranian version of Yeonmi Park, the North
Korean propagandist for US conservative reactionaries. They are
made of the same cloth: with minimal factual connections to their

147

homelands, they are used to demonize US adversaries through the reassuring foreign accent of a native informer.[1] Both Alinejad and Park operate like ChatGPT or any other AI software that is preprogrammed to spin certain propaganda lines just like an old-fashioned broken record.

Alinejad detests the Islamic Republic, and the feeling is mutual. Alinejad uses the internet and social media to attack and demonize the Islamic Republic (not that it needed to be demonized more than it actually is) and the Islamic Republic returns the favor. There are reports that the ruling regime in Iran has plotted to kidnap or even kill her.[2] She has both weaponized and transformed that threat into a lucrative business deal for herself. According to reports, a US court has mandated that Iran pay Alinejad $3.3 million in damages.[3] "A judge representing the United States District Court for the District of Columbia," reports *Middle East Eye*, "awarded Masih, a US-based campaigner against compulsory headscarves in Iran, $1,662,500 in compensatory damages and $1,662,500 in punitive damages, after ruling in her favor and against the Islamic Republic of Iran."[4] It is a freak show: between the propaganda machinery of the Islamic Republic and the propaganda machinery that stages Alinejad as a bona fide leader of the opposition. All of that engineered and manufactured online, in the mindless, heartless, chaotic confusions of cyberspace.

THE PERILS AND PROMISES OF CYBERSPACE

Is there any correspondence between factual, verifiable truth and the propaganda that Masih Alinejad or Yeonmi Park let loose on the internet? There was a time when social media—Facebook,

Twitter, and now especially Instagram for Iranians—was considered to be a revolutionary development that could be put squarely at the service of democratic uprisings. During the Egyptian revolution there were reports that people were naming their newborns "Facebook."[5] It turned out that these platforms are actually not such great news, for the ruling states were also using the selfsame machineries to propagate their own lies, demonize their enemies, spy on them, and arrest, harass, torture, jail, defame, and silence them. The Israeli spyware Pegasus became infamous for putting such technology, used to spy on enemies of the state, at the disposal of repressive regimes to frighten and eliminate their defiant citizens. Israelis have practice on this front, experimenting with their captured population of Palestinians. In his book *Net Delusion: The Dark Side of Internet Freedom* (2012), Evgeny Morozov has demonstrated, with plenty of references to Iran, that the revolution will not be tweeted, that the initial optimism of claiming that these software gadgets would help the world take that final democratic turn were highly exaggerated. Regimes like Iran and China were in fact turning the tables on the internet and using it to stabilize themselves, demonize their nemeses, and launch malware against other states. During Donald Trump's first presidential campaign, there were consistent reports that Russians were using disinformation on the internet to help him defeat Hillary Clinton.[6] Instead of opposing or curtailing the internet, states were turning it into to the "Spinternet," according to Morozov:

> It's hardly surprising, then, that authoritarian governments from Russia to Iran and from China to Azerbaijan are busy turning the Internet into the Spinternet—a Web with little censorship but lots of spin and propaganda—which reinforces their ideological supremacy. The age of

new media, with its characteristic fragmentation of public discourse and decentralization of control, has made the lives of propaganda officials toiling in stuffy offices of authoritarian governments considerably easier.[7]

As Masih Alinejad was being programmed and unleashed on the Islamic Republic, with US-based Zionist enterprises leading the way, giving her prizes, and cheering her on, and as glossy magazines kept pace by featuring her on covers, the Islamic Republic was busy doing the same against her and all other internet-based cyber celebrities. Caught in between Ali Khamenei on one side and Masih Alinejad on the other were the ordinary people, both subjected and unsusceptible to their self-serving propaganda—Alinejad to secure a lucrative spot for her brand of celebrity, and Khamenei to keep the machinery of a murderous theocracy running smoothly. But where was the truth? What was the real nature of the Zhina uprising? On the gravesite of young protesters murdered by the security forces of the ruling regime? On university campuses, where students were screaming obscenities against Khamenei? In the streets of Baluchistan and Kurdistan, filled with real people with real pains and their handwritten signs against tyranny? Or online, on the social media accounts of Alinejad and Khamenei? With barefaced vulgarity, Alinejad was able to convince a seasoned journalist like Dexter Filkins of the *New Yorker* that she was the real leader of the Zhina uprising.[8] Who was to tell Filkins, writing for one of the most respected icons of liberalism in the United States, that a rank charlatan had taken him and his readers for a ridiculous ride?

Entirely against the grain of varied social formations for civil disobedience within Iran, led by real people, is the massive but vacuous force of social media where celebrity activists, as they are dubbed, are the unreal products of this deceptive environment and have a heyday on the Iranian political scene. We need to understand the illusory force of how social media works in this context, generating the delusion of a phantom liberty that has little to do with the actual lived experiences of people in the streets, alleys, squares, schools, factories, mosques, hospitals, and university campuses in Iran. This is particularly acute in the case of expat activists in the United States, Canada, Australia, and Europe who scarce have a factual reality outside the hall of mirrors that internet activism has falsely generated for them.

Celebrity activists, to be sure, are a symptom, not the actual disease. The actual disease is the Islamic Republic itself, the absence of freedom of expression, freedom of peaceful assembly, and freedom of the press inside Iran, where leading investigative journalists like Akbar Ganji have been sentenced to excruciating jail sentences and their barely breathing bodies (after a prolonged hunger strike that almost killed him) are left to languish in exile. The ruling Islamist regime has total and totalitarian control over the means of mass media. The internet is severely controlled and abused against dissidents. People have had no choice but to run to social media, which has its own logic and madness. This creates cyberspace celebrities who are in turn under the illusion that they actually represent something. Meanwhile, foreign outlets like Voice of America or BBC Persian are also widely popular in and outside Iran, for they successfully fake an autonomy which they lack, for they represent the best interests of US and UK state policies. Saudi Arabia has actively financed sold-out expat Iranian journalists (who are not qualified to work for any decent media outlet) and puts them to use to generate propaganda against and instigate the Islamic Republic. These factors have severely compromised cyberspace, where the louder and more obscene a voice, the wider its appeal to keyboard activists, cyberbullies, bots, and their pestiferous algorithms.

The result of this circus is a foregone conclusion. Here is an example. On New Year's Eve in 2023, the late Shah's son Reza Pahlavi and a number of other cyber celebrities who had placed their bets on a defeated monarchy published an identical text on their respective social media accounts wishing their followers success in the new Christian year, promising crucial changes in the year ahead in the fate of their homeland.[9] What was peculiar about this message was that it had been timed to the Christian calendar, not the Iranian or Islamic calendar. Equally crucial was the enormous cyberspace (phantasmagoric) popularity of those who had joined the Pahlavi bid to return to the peacock throne, including figures like the Paris-based Iranian actress Golshifteh Farahani, the con artist Alinejad, and popular footballer Ali Karimi. Not to be left behind, other reactionary monarchists based at a neocon joint on the Stanford University campus upped the ante and invited even more internet-savvy characters to announce their version of the "passage to democracy." No sane person would chase after such fake news except to document the systematic ways in which a genuine social uprising in Iran—an uprising code-named Mahsa or Zhina after its first victim—was being consistently manhandled to fit the reactionary interests of American right-wing politics. Iranian expats had become increasingly like those Cubans who had left their homeland in the aftermath of the Cuban revolution and were now siding with the most reactionary US forces against their own homeland.

We might also consider such cyberspace spectacles as the latest manifestations of the post-politics of the culture industry. The internet is mass deception, of the sort that Theodor Adorno and Max Horkheimer could never have dreamed in the 1940s.[10] According to a major study by an Iranian social scientist, the most popular figures on Iranian Instagram were actors, musicians, and athletes—namely celebrity activists.[11] This entirely internet-based popularity—fake yet overwhelming and, as such, definitive to the expat Iranian keyboard activists—had by now compromised the global reading of the Zhina uprising. First and foremost is the key issue of the "culture industry," as Adorno and Horkheimer theorized it soon after World War II, when they believed the greatest danger to a potent political consciousness in American democracy lay in the mass-culture apparatus of film, radio, and television. But things have become far more sinister since the time of Adorno and Horkheimer, and the era of celebrity activists feeds into what leading scholars of the information technology now call "surveillance capitalism." The culture industry has by now ceased to serve global capitalism. It has become global capitalism.

The single common denominator of characters like Golshifteh Farahani, Masih Alinejad, Nazanin Boniadi, Ali Karimi, and Hamed Esmaeilion is the fact they are all phantom celebrity activists, known not because of their actual leadership in any political capacity inside or outside Iran but as hologram simulacra of actors, footballers, agent provocateurs, or, in the case of Esmaeilion, a bereaved father and husband whose family perished when the Iranians downed a commercial airliner on January 8, 2021, mistaking it for a US attack. Whatever their factual presence in real life might be, of which the world knew little before they began speaking for the Zhina uprising, their delusional persona in cyberspace became symptomatic of an irreality that generates and sustains the false apparition of reality. The eminent French sociologist Jean Baudrillard (1929–2007), in his pioneering book

Simulacra and Simulation (1981) and later in *The Gulf War Did Not Take Place* (1991), detailed the power of such hyperrealities. In the following passage (written originally in French in 1981, translated later into English in 1994) Baudrillard (entirely unbeknownst to himself) was anticipating and describing Masih Alinejad, before anyone except her parents knew the child they named Masoumeh Alinejad-Ghomikolayi:

> To dissimulate is to pretend not to have what one has. To simulate is to feign to have what one hasn't. One implies a presence, the other an absence. But it is more complicated than that because simulating is not pretending: "Whoever fakes an illness can simply stay to bed and make everyone believe he is ill. Whoever simulates an illness produces in himself some of the symptoms." . . . Therefore, pretending, or dissimulating leaves the principle of reality intact: the difference is always clear, it is simply masked, whereas simulation threatens the difference between the "true" and the "false," the "real" and the "imaginary." Is the simulator sick or not, given that he produces "true" symptoms? Objectively one cannot treat him as being either ill or not ill. Psychology and medicine stop at this point, forestalled by the illness's henceforth undiscoverable truth.[12]

Alinejad feigned to have led this uprising from the safe and ridiculous distance of the United States—and anything she said became a simulacrum of truth. All critical judgments were dubbed "leftist" and thus suspect. But, as Baudrillard says, the phenomenon was even more complicated than a mere chase for ignorant US journalists in search of yet another Aung San Suu Kyi (flower in the hair and all). They found her, themselves, and the world believing that she was the real thing, the leader of this uprising. The hyperreality she staged about the Zhina uprising on the internet had overcome the reality of it. This was the age of post-truth. Is Alinejad real, or is she a hologram, a computer-generated bot—and what difference does it make? The Islamic Republic had created a Frankenstein monster in evident opposition to itself and yet in its own image: frightful, unreal, but with terribly material consequences.

SURVEILLANCE CAPITALISM

How does this surveillance capitalism feed into the provenance of hologram celebrity activists creating the delusion of political activism on the ground? In an essay in the *New York Times*, Shoshana Zuboff, a professor emeritus at Harvard Business School and author of *The Age of Surveillance Capitalism* (2019), has provided some key insights with reference to the attempted coup by then-president Donald Trump on January 6, 2021.[13] She writes that there is a "coup we are not talking about," by which she means the rise of what she calls "surveillance society" and an "information civilization" predicated on her analysis of surveillance capitalism. In this information civilization, surveillance capitalists, like Google and Facebook, are those who decide who knows what, from which she concludes: "The horrific depths of Donald Trump's attempted political coup ride the wave of this shadow coup, prosecuted over the last two decades by the antisocial media we once welcomed as agents of liberation."[14] Echoing the insights of Evgeny Morozov in his *Net Delusion*, Zuboff confirms that the pipe dream of social media, which she rightly calls "antisocial media," being an instrument of liberation is its opposite. This shadow coup is what Zuboff calls an "epistemic coup" in which she shows how surveillance capitalism may abuse people's lives as private corporate property. Iranian expat cyberspace celebrities are extending the logic of surveillance capitalism, turning the heroic sacrifices of a young generation into raw material at the service of not just the United States, but the Islamic Republic itself, and in turn Israeli spyware companies, as to how to control, manipulate, and reverse the impact of the data they will have collected. In other words, the factual evidence of the Zhina uprising, through the manufactured popularity of such holograph activists, becomes the raw data in reversing its course and doing precisely the opposite of its stated intentions. "People's lives as free raw material." Where have we heard that before? All the subsequent stages Zuboff describes correspond to a colonial condition that was not of much concern to her but should be to us. Paradoxically, or perhaps not, it was the events of 9/11 that triggered governments to start harvesting for mass surveillance—initially of Muslims but eventually everyone. The roots of this intelligence gathering or surveillance colonialism are not limited to Iran or Arabs or Muslims and extend far wider, from India to Africa to Latin America and even Europe itself. Both capitalism and colonialism do not just need intelligence. They manufacture what they need and stage it as truth. We can go back to Napoleon's invasion of Egypt in 1798, when he had commissioned a group of Orientalists to accompany his army to produce the kind of knowledge he needed to conquer, and justify conquering, an Arab country. The knowledge and artifacts the French collected (stole) from Egypt and other African countries became the very foundation of French and other European museums of antiquities and university departments of archaeology and anthropology. Egyptology was a colonial discipline at its roots. Today, however, the situation is out of control. These Iranian celebrity activists online demonstrate how vacuous and yet how powerful these delusional fantasies garbed as truth are. But even more importantly, the fake "data" they collect and falsely identify as truth becomes the material at the disposal of surveillance capitalists to monitor, control, and subvert real social movements like the Zhina uprising.

What began as Orientalism abroad soon came home to Europe and the United States to roost. Before long, Europe itself would become the site of intelligence gathering for the CIA, which was worried about the worldwide appeal of the cultural left. Gabriel Rockhill, in a 2017 essay for the *Los Angeles Review of Books*, "The CIA Reads French Theory: On the Intellectual Labor of Dismantling the Cultural Left," detailed US intelligence officers trying to figure out what leading French critical thinkers like Michel Foucault, Jacques Lacan, and Roland Barthes were all up to.[15] When the selfsame critical thinkers, especially Foucault, became instrumental in Edward Said's subsequent exposure of Orientalism as the modus operandi of colonial knowledge and power, it was now the turn of American Zionists like Bernard Lewis and his minions to attack Said, and the entire field of postcolonial studies he helped establish, for their crucial role in exposing the machinations of Israel. The Orient of the Orientalists was surveillance society long before the term was coined to understand capitalism in the United States and Europe. Now, these hologram Iranian celebrity activists are claiming and distorting the Zhina movement, linking the self-Orientalization of a grassroots uprising to the surveillance capitalism at the heart of US and EU foreign policies. Definitive to that delusional movement is when Alinejad and her ilk take a selfie with French President Emmanuel Macron and put it on their Instagram accounts. The hologram with a flower in her newly unveiled hair seeks radically to redefine and attach herself to a grassroots movement for which the young and old Kurds and Baluch are shedding their blood in a faraway real world. In a sense Alinejad is correct: she is the leader of the Zhina uprising when it has grotesquely metamorphosed from a factual reality in the streets and squares of Iran into a digitized delusion on Instagram, Twitter, and other antisocial media.

The irreality that we see amounts to an epistemic coup in our reading of reality—not just about how our mass data can be used and abused but also in how the internet generates a fundamentally flipped, topsy-turvy perception of reality and posits it in lieu of reality. The late Palestinian scholar Elia Zureik and his colleagues have detailed the Israeli technologies of surveillance and biopolitics in the brutal strategies of population control in occupied Palestine.[16] There is a reason why Israel is a "hub for surveillance technology," and engaged in "selling its products around the world to governments that want to spy on their own citizens."[17] Understanding what is happening inside the United States in the twenty-first century is contingent on understanding what the US and its favorite garrison state—and long before them their European colonial forebears—have done around the globe. And understanding that genealogy is a solid base from which to see how celebrity activism and surveillance capitalism are integral to each other and how they necessitate, corroborate, and promote each other.

Shoshana Zuboff speaks of an epistemic coup that unfolds in four stages: (1) appropriation of epistemic rights; (2) a sharp rise in epistemic inequality; (3) introduction of epistemic chaos; and (4) epistemic dominance, which is driven to override democratic governance. The way we postcolonials have mapped out precisely these stages in our own words and risen up to oppose and end them contains a crucial lesson for scholars like Professor Zuboff who are deeply concerned—as she rightly is—about how to oppose and end this barbaric domination. To see the roots of surveillance capitalism in surveillance colonialism, the first place to start is to reread Edward Said's *Orientalism* (1978) through Zuboff's perceptive eyes. The most rudimentary lesson of that rereading of *Orientalism* in post-Trump America is that Americans cannot engage in surveillance imperialism around the globe and be the key patron of their favorite settler colony (as it engages in surveillance colonialism in Palestine) while seeking to overcome surveillance capitalism at home. But equally crucial is that when rooted social movements like the Zhina uprising are appropriated by the symptoms of surveillance capitalism in the form of celebrity activists, who owe their celebrity status almost exclusively to manipulated algorithms, their cyberspace popularity generates its own vacuous, unreal, and mass criteria of alternative facts and delusional fantasies.

AN EXTENDED WEB OF GROUP AFFILIATIONS

While the mass-scale cyberspace trolling and the celebrity holograms it generates and promotes are entirely detrimental to any serious democratic cause, one should not completely ignore the potential uses of social media and the way its small-scale integration into preexisting and real social formations remains healthy and necessary. Neither enamored by the phantasmagoric promises of social networking of the digital age nor antiquarian, we could alternatively think of a more robust and healthier fusion of the two when social media becomes part of physical social life. Since the Green Movement of 2009 and the Arab Spring of 2010, I have been writing about social media as integral to Georg Simmel's idea of "the web of group affiliation," where we are part of a network of concentric circles consisting of family, friends, colleagues, neighborhoods, churches, synagogues, mosques, university fraternities, labor unions, and professional associations—anywhere an individual might belong and thereby find their social character. Here is a key passage from Simmel's 1922 essay:

> The number of different social groups in which the individual participates, is one of the earmarks of culture. The modern person belongs first to his parental family, then to his family of procreation and thereby also to the family of his wife. Beyond this he belongs to his occupational group, which often involves him in several interest groups. . . . Moreover, a person also participates in a group made up of similarly situated employees from several different firms. Then a person is likely to be aware of his citizenship, of the fact that he belongs to a particular social group. . . . The modern type of group formation makes it possible for the isolated individual to become a member in whatever number of groups he chooses.[18]

The internet age has created a new transnational culture where an individual may sit in New York and be part of an online community that includes people from around the globe—some of whom may be entirely fictional but still compelling. The group affiliations that Simmel outlines remain valid today, and so far as an Instagram, Twitter, or Facebook are not the totality of a person's existence and, as in the case of celebrity holographs, have not assumed a life of their own, one can see the way, as Simmel believed, a person "regains his individuality" by virtue of adding just one element to the existing pattern of their group affiliation. The problem with celebrity activists is that this cyber hyperreality overwhelms and replaces everything else. One might also consider social media as part of the larger public sphere in which a private person becomes a social persona by virtue of participation in a larger frame of social reference. In my previous work I have articulated the existence of a "parapublic sphere,"[19] such as underground publications, prisons, and clandestine groups, to which we might also add an email list-serv, a Facebook page or a Twitter or Instagram account.

The point here is simple: by now the widespread existence of social networking in cyberspace is a technological fact of life full of hazards and illusions, hope and despair. But at the same time, it has also enabled a level of transnational communication and formation of social solidarity never before imagined. At the best and most hopeful moments of the Green Movement and the Arab Spring, such communications were effective in actual popular mobilization in Azadi or Tahrir squares in Tehran and Cairo, respectively. But by the time we reached the Zhina uprising in September 2022, the rise of cyberspace celebrities had overwhelmed and replaced the factual, material, and healthy public sphere with delusional and dangerous celebrity holograms that were pulling these movements into a politics of mass society, as William Kornhauser called it in his 1959 classic,[20] where moral imagination and political commitment had degenerated into delusional fantasies of effectively atomized individuals quixotically leading shadow armies of internet trolls to fictional victories. The same element of social anomie generated by the ruling tyrannies might lead to social movements enjoying a brief moment of false Gemeinschaft, then soon resuming its habitual anomie and pursuing the course of social susceptibility to the next totalitarian turn. For healthy and robust social uprisings like Zhina to sustain their prolonged political impact, the degeneration of the realities they entail into unreal simulation of the politics of mass society and cyberspace vacuity must be opposed like a plague. This is the single most enduring lesson of career opportunist cyber trolls like Alinejad or Yeonmi Park—particularly incubated in the reactionary politics of right-wing dilettantism of the Trumpian United States.

SEVEN

RETURN OF THE PAHLAVIS WITH A VENGEANCE

Salaam... Salaam, Morad baz ham peidat shod...
Morad, you again? Did I not tell you time and again.....
What can I do Shazdeh? I can't make ends meet! When I
realized we don't have food to eat tonight I said: Hasani
bring me the wheelchair, perhaps the generosity of the
Shazdeh might come to our aid.

—**Bahman Farmanara** (1974)

"First of all allow me to say as a political prisoner I am opposed to any kind of repression, imprisonment, solitary confinement, torture, or execution."[1] Thus begins the letter Bahareh Soleimani, a political prisoner, sent from her cell in the notorious Evin Prison on January 23, 2023. From here she proceeds to write that she will defend the right of any human being and any political prisoner to believe in whatever they believe. Nevertheless, she wishes to share some of her experiences in the women's ward of the Evin Prison. She says before she went to jail she had no experience with Iranian monarchists, had only witnessed their thuggish behaviors on social media, and had thought this was just characteristic of that particular virtual space. But much to her regret she has had to spend her time in jail with them and has had to endure their politics and behavior.

> I can boldly state I have never seen a people more unethi-
> cal, immoral, and illiterate than these monarchists. . . . They
> believe all political activists during the Pahlavi period were
> terrorists and murderers. . . . They believe the great poet
> Ahmad Shamlou was an apostate and committed treason for
> having composed poems for those executed under the Pahla-
> vis. They believe the Pahlavis had made the Evin Prison for
> terrorists and they did a good thing when they did so.[2]

She then writes of these political prisoners' unabashed racism and xenophobia against the Afghan refugees, whom they call "Afghan dogs" and "backward Afghans." If others were to accuse them of being fascists, they say that yes, they are fascists and proud of it. They say so not because they are angry with others, they just are fascist. They watch television and cheer when neo-Nazis win elections in Europe. They admire Hitler for having considered the Aryan race the superior race. They repeat the slogan initiated by their monarchists in London: "Death to the three corrupts: the mullahs, the left, the mojaheds." The spouse of Reza Pahlavi, Yasmine Pahlavi—or "the Queen," as the monarchists call her—has tweeted the same slogan.

The Pahlavi dynasty (1925 to 1979)—now overthrown and represented by Reza Pahlavi (born 1960), the crown prince under the deposed monarchy, and his elder mother, Farah (Diba) Pahlavi, the former queen, all of them based in the United States—actively returned to the political scene with a vengeance soon after the commencement of the Zhina uprising. Reza Pahlavi had always been passively present over the last four decades after the demise of the Pahlavis. But by and large he led a lucrative, quiet family life—entirely hopeless and useless in political terms. The memory of his father, the late Mohammad Reza Shah (who reigned from 1941 to 1979) has, however, become increasingly popular, especially among a younger generation of Iranians systematically abused by the Islamist regime. The widespread social protests that engulfed Iran in the fall of 2022 suddenly gave both Reza Pahlavi and a group of repressed, angry, vindictive, and exceedingly loud, vulgar, and unabashedly fascist followers a new lease on life. It has been surreal to see monarchists in the streets and squares of the United States and Europe rooting for their deposed dynasty, as if nothing has happened over the last half a century. It would be a mistake to dismiss the entirety of the Pahlavi cause as those of militant monarchists. The family, especially the late Shah and his Queen Farah, do command genuine affection by considerable swaths of Iranian people—in part out of a rooted hatred of the Islamic Republic, in part out of an ahistorical nostalgia for pre-revolution Iran. The memory of Iran under the Pahlavis is now the site of contestation between the Pahlavi monarchists and their dubious claim to the future of Iranian history.

THINKING LIKE AN AMERICAN POLITICIAN

The Pahlavis came to power with a military coup in 1925. They were soon deposed by a military occupation in 1941, reinstituted by the selfsame military occupation, challenged by a democratic uprising in 1951, restored back to power by a military coup to dismantle that democratic uprising in 1953, and yet again deposed by a widely popular revolution from 1977 to 1979. That history, detailed and documented, is today overwhelmed by a fake and fanatical attack orchestrated by deposed and discredited but determined expat monarchists dead set to use and abuse the chaotic thunderbox of social media to rewrite Iran's history. To be sure, the Pahlavis are not without their supporters inside Iran among a disaffected portion of the population that so detests the Islamic Republic and that has nostalgia for the *ancien régime*. But this militant Pahlavism is largely an expat phenomenon. The problem with Reza Pahlavi is the fact that both his grandfather and his father were forced into exile, one by an allied occupation and the other by a historic revolutionary mobilization, just a couple of decades after the Shah of Shahs had run away from a democratically elected anticolonial politician, Mohammad Mosaddegh, who was not beholden to the British and the Americans. This historic trauma afflicts Reza Pahlavi, now in his early sixties, not by any political party to which he might be accountable but against the very grain of Iranian history. He has lived much of his adult life in the United States. It is normal for his very political character and culture to have been affected by American politics.

The militant Pahlavism that was resurrected mostly (but not entirely) in the United States soon after the Zhina uprising was a godsend for the ruling Islamist regime—for it seemed to have divided the opposition along some serious lines: reverting back to a defeated and outdated dynasty, or moving forward beyond the calamities of a decrepit theocracy and the monarchy it had overthrown. But this was a false reading of the uprising, for militant Pahlavism was mostly an internet phenomenon, engineered in the United States, where the Pahlavis had opted to wed their politics to the right wing of the Republican Party, which included "Make Persia Great Again" versions of the MAGA hats—and a bizarre trip to Israel. Reza Pahlavi and his wife, Yasmine, traveled to Israel in April 2023 by way of pos-

ing himself as the leader of the Zhina uprising. This was a truly outlandish move, for the picture of Reza Pahlavi standing next to Israeli
Prime Minister Benjamin Netanyahu was worse than the picture of
Massoud Rajavi, the Mujaheddin-e Khalq (MEK) leader, sitting next
to Saddam Hussein back in 1987 as he waged a war against Iran. The
widely circulated picture was a sign of the complete Americanization
of Reza Pahlavi, as if he was running for office in some district in
Washington, DC, with a major Zionist constituency.[3]

Neither Israel nor, in fact, Palestine is an important issue in the
Zhina uprising. There are, of course, enduring and profound roots
in a sustained solidarity with the Palestinians in Iran going back
to 1948 and the Nakba because of its own anticolonial struggles
that long predate the establishment of the settler colony of Israel
and the dispossession of Palestinians. But at the same time there
are also those Iranians who so detest the ruling regime in Iran that
they extend that hatred to places like Palestine, Lebanon, Syria, or
Yemen, where the ruling regime has expanded its theater of oper-
ations. Reza Pahlavi was taken for a ride by his American Zionist
handlers, who snapped his photo at the Wailing Wall (a perfectly
fine thing to do), when, as a Muslim, he failed to even look up the
location of Haram al-Sharif, where, just a few days before his igno-
minious visit, the Israeli police had savagely attacked praying Palestinians. Reza Pahlavi is a Muslim, named after the eighth Shi'i
Imam, who is buried in Iran, and he has a claim to leading a Muslim
country to freedom, and yet he seemed so utterly alien to his most
natural home and habitat. The problem with Reza Pahlavi is that he
now appeared as a banal and clichéd American politician in search
of a royal prototype. He has spent his entire adult life in exile from
his homeland and has had a private and mostly happy life, though
marked by the tragedy of two of his siblings committing suicide.

Far from this pitiful tempest in a teapot, we need to distinguish among a number of conflated facts and factors here: first, the ruling Islamist regime in Iran has from its very birth been detested by significant parts of the population they wish to rule, especially in poverty-stricken areas like Sistan and Baluchistan or Iranian Kurdistan and among the victims of rampant corruption and elitism in the Islamic Republic; second, the current legitimate revolt known as the Zhina uprising is based on deep-rooted economic, social and political conditions; and finally, there is a freak show of expat opposition forces like the monarchists, US-Israeli-sponsored regime changers, and, until recently, Saudi-supported agitators like MEK. In the rise of militant Pahlavism we were witnessing a mirror image of something we have seen before. The same way that the rise of militant Islamism was a by-product of Pahlavi tyranny, today the rise of militant Pahlavism is the direct consequence of the militant Islamism that has ruled Iran vindictively for nearly half a century. Were it not for the terror that the Islamic Republic has inflicted upon the country from its very inception, the Pahlavi monarchists would not have had the audacity and barefaced vulgarity to so thoroughly disregard even the most recent history and demand a political return to power.

HISTORICAL AMNESIA

When Parviz Sabeti suddenly surfaced in pro-Pahlavi demonstrations in the United States in February 2023, the signs of a pathological amnesia in the historical memory, or else a manifestation of thumbing one's nose at it, became too vulgar to ignore.[4] Sabeti was perhaps the most detested public face of SAVAK, the dreaded secret police of the Pahlavi regime—reportedly created by the CIA and the Mossad soon after the monarchy was restored to power following the CIA-MI6 coup of 1953. An entire generation of political activists remember the dreaded name and despise the lasting memory of Sabeti. And now, right from the heart of the Zhina uprising, that ghostly apparition had come back to haunt them. "I thought this was unbelievable," a former political prisoner told Al Jazeera upon seeing a picture of Sabeti at a rally. "When I saw him [Sabeti], it was like he was mocking us. The beatings, the torture, it all came back. It was like I was in jail all over again."[5] Reza Pahlavi was resurrecting these ghosts. There was no separating the Pahlavi dynasty from the frightful memories of its repressive security apparatus and the fear and loathing it had left behind in the collective memories of a nation. Yes, the Islamic Republic had done worse than the Pahlavis in these terms, and successive reports by Amnesty International and Human Rights Watch had documented that fact. But right from the heart of the most hopeful uprising had now emerged the most hateful names associated with the Pahlavi regime. After almost half a century, it was still too soon to forget these names and yet too late to restore legitimacy to the monarchy, which was founded on systematic fear and intimidation.

There is a fundamental difference between Reza Pahlavi and his father, it had now become quite evident. Mohammad Reza Shah was born to an established monarchy, raised as a crown prince, and attended a finishing school in Switzerland. His father was overthrown by Allied forces when his pro-Nazi sentiments became evident, and Mohammad Reza Shah was then installed in power with the full support of the United States and the UK. Reza Pahlavi's life began in a similar way, but he was still a teenager when he was forced into exile by the widely popular revolution of 1977 to 1979. His father was brought back to power via a military coup in 1953, and he was therefore used to being supported by superpowers.[6] The late Shah was therefore confident in his actions, and even a widely popular prime minister like Mohammad Mosaddegh could not shake his confidence. Reza Pahlavi lacks both that confidence and that lived experience of his late royal father. Compared to Reza Shah, even the Shah was a weakling, and now, compared with his father, Reza Pahlavi looked positively like an American politician without his own constituency. The central trauma of the dynasty is their point of origin in a military officer named Reza Khan. Khan was brought to power by the British to put an end to the varied democratic uprisings around the country. Aided and abetted by the British through their agent Edmund Ironside (1880–1959), Reza Khan (as he was known at the time) staged a military coup on February 21, 1921, when his comrade and rival Zia al-Din Tabataba'i (1889–1969) became prime minister. From that moment forward, the fate of the Qajars was doomed, as the rise of Reza Khan to power was rooted in his political ambitions as the head of the Persian Cossack Brigade, with Prime Minister Zia al-Din Tabataba'i as his co-conspirator to topple the Qajars. Reza Khan's active militarism won the rivalry and prepared him to succeed as the next strongman approved by the British. By 1923 Reza Khan had assumed a national military role and soon after he became prime minister under the last Qajar monarch, Ahmad Shah, who, before long, ran away to Europe. Reza Khan was now officially in charge of the country. By October 1925, he engineered the overthrow of the Qajars, and his rise as the next monarch was sealed. The Majlis did his bidding and rubber-stamped the new monarch on December 12, 1925. He coronated himself as the king the following year on April 25, 1926.[7]

With that active memory of the origin of the dynasty, the problem with the return of the Pahlavis to the political scene in the midst of the Zhina uprising is their outdated currency, rooted in the collapse of their monarchy in the late 1970s. After the demise of the Pahlavis,

Iran has gone through the hellfire of an Islamic republic. In that fire have burned the foundational legitimacies of both the mullarchy that has ruled over Iran and the monarchy it had succeeded. What has remained is the revolutionary zeal of the 1970s being repeatedly rekindled by subsequent generations over the last four decades by social and economic factors. The Pahlavis were never part of those revolutionary momentums. They have lacked institutional legitimacy and they have failed to be represented by a charismatic leader. Reza Pahlavi is a suburban family man being goaded into assuming a revolutionary role he has no clue how to play—now democratic, now autocratic, now popular, now royal. The absence of legitimacy for the Pahlavis does not translate into legitimacy for the Islamic Republic and its outdated theocracy, which is held in power by the sheer violence of its military, security, and intelligence apparatus. In its momentum and significance, the Zhina uprising is overcoming all institutional claims to political authority, beginning with the Islamic Republic itself and a fortiori all the previous dynastic claims it has swallowed.

COMMODIFYING THE ZHINA UPRISING

The problem with the Pahlavis is not just their recent history. It is also in their imagined future—how the monarchists envision themselves in a future country. Because of them, a profoundly reactionary force is at work within the Zhina uprising—marked by its rapid commodification by some well-known monarchists. Bold and banal eroticization of the uprising was championed early in the movement by such leading activists as the France-based actresses Golshifteh Farahani and Zar Amir Ebrahimi, whose photos soon began to pop up on glossy magazines promoting their take on the event. "This is not a revolt," they declared loud and clear on the cover of a French magazine, "this is a revolution." The erotic commodification of the Zhina uprising consolidated the European male gaze cast upon it—and with it the potent patriarchy that had occasioned it—and went, with no sense of irony, precisely against the very logic of the "Zan, Zendegi, Azadi" slogan. The look, the gaze, and the spectacle were all light years from the impoverished women of Baluchistan, with 70 percent of them living beneath the poverty line, or the Kulbars in the mountains of Kurdistan risking their lives for a meager living smuggling illegal goods. Farahani, Amir Ebrahimi, Masih Alinejad, and Shahin Najafi became emblematic of a resurgent Pahlavi neoliberalism that sought revenge against not just the Islamists who had succeeded them but the very 1977 to 1979 revolution that had been a turning point in modern Iranian history. It was hard to decide which part of it was scarier: banality, boredom, illiteracy, or the scarce hidden fascism they all unabashedly staged. When the picture of the widely popular pop singer Googoosh showed up on a billboard that read "Zan, Zendegi, Azadi" to sell her perfume, the cycle of a coarse, callous, and vulgar commodification was complete.

Through such figures as Googoosh and Farahani, the Women, Life, Freedom uprising was actively and consistently eroticized, commercialized, commodified, and thereby reified and fetishized, entirely divorced from the lived realities that had given rise to that uprising. Based in California or France, these figures, sporting a rich and insular life, were integral either to the expat Iranian communities or else part of the French chic in need of an Oriental spin on the products they were selling. But what were they selling aside from their own art, names, or reputations? Here, as advocates of the Zhina uprising, they were selling something else. Through their commodification of a massive social uprising far removed from their own lives, they were actively transforming it into an object of trade and commerce. Anything and everything was for sale—including the Zhina uprising and the "Zan, Zendegi, Azadi" slogan. The fetishizing of this commodity was manifold, particularly in the eroticization, Orientalization, and exoticization of the Zhina event, in effect selling the uprising as a desirable product to their European and American interlocutors and consumers. They were giving new meaning and significance to Marx's classical reading of commodity fetishism in the first volume of *Capital* (1867).

> A commodity is therefore a mysterious thing, simply because in it the social character of men's labor appears to them as an objective character stamped upon the product of that labor; because the relation of the producers to the sum total of their own labor is presented to them as a social relation, existing not between themselves, but between the products of their labor. This is the reason why the products of labor become commodities, social things whose qualities are at the same time perceptible and imperceptible by the senses. . . . In order, therefore, to find an analogy, we must have recourse to the mist-enveloped regions of the religious world. In that world the productions of the human brain appear as independent beings endowed with life, and entering into relation both with one another and the human race. So it is in the world of commodities with the products of men's hands. This I call the Fetishism which attaches itself to the products of labor, so soon as they are produced as commodities, and which is therefore inseparable from the production of commodities.[8]

The same is true with the manner in which the Zhina uprising in Iran is being actively commodified halfway around the world, bought and sold, and symbolically fetishized as something to be possessed, either as pictures of two actively Orientalized young Iranian women or else a perfume attached to the name of widely popular entertainer Googoosh. Farahani's and Ebrahimi's photographed bodies and Googoosh's perfume have become the commodified simulacra of the Zhina uprising, standing for and selling a massive social movement completely removed from these transactions.[9] You buy these glossy magazines and look at these pictures, or else you buy that perfume and smell and wear it, and there, there you have the Zhina uprising in a nutshell, as it were—digested, consumed, bought and sold, done with.[10] The truth and reality and the harsh lived experiences of men, women, and children suffering the horrors of a corrupt and incompetent Islamic republic are here radically altered and fetishized into these lively-looking commodities readily available for sale. Such transactions are rooted in the neoliberal economics the Pahlavi cause was staging in the US and European markets that are far removed from the epicenter of the Zhina uprising, an uprising by millions of impoverished and brutalized people. This is the image the Pahlavis have imagined for the future of Iran. It starts not with facts on the ground, but with the global market of neoliberal economics, even before Reza Pahlavi has set foot back in Iran and come anywhere near power, wedding the fate of some eighty million human beings to neoliberal economics, globalized politics, and their corresponding culture industries.

WHEN ART HAUNTS HISTORY

The Pahlavis are a lost cause, even in more rooted cultural terms. Consider one of the most iconic events on the cultural scene before the Islamists commandeered the Iranian Revolution of 1977 to 1979. Houshang Golshiri's masterpiece *Prince Ehtejab* (1968) was the artistic finale to the story of a Persian monarchy left in ruins— not just the Qajars or the Pahlavis but the entire institution of monarchy.[11] The introverted and convoluted memorial narrative of the novella sucks the reader into its phantasmagoric prose with no choice but to breathe its musty air. Dark and foreboding, the prince's recollections of the Qajar cruelties oscillate between the shades and shadows of his and our consciousnesses, the light and darkness of our haunted history. The novella became the most psychologically potent account of the demise and fall of the Qajar monarchy. Standing for all princes before and after him, Prince Ehtejab lives inside the toxic tonality of his own hallucinations, and with his recollections all of history has become hallucinatory. *Prince Ehtejab* has been rightly compared to Sadegh Hedayat's *The Blind Owl* (1936) and Sadegh Chubak's *Tangsir* (1963) as master- pieces of Persian fiction. After Hedayat's *The Blind Owl*, Golshiri's prose stages the most formidable formal presence of Persian dic- tion, in which the three characters of Prince Ehtejab, his wife Prin- cess Fakhr al-Nisa, and their servant Fakhri all become one. In a similar tone, *Prince Ehtejab* conflates the Qajars and the Pahlavis and from that mixture recasts the history of Iranian monarchy, reaching for the psychotic disposition of despotism and cruelty at the heart of all hereditary power. Both the prince and his wife are dying, physically and symbolically, while the prince's obses- sion with his wife and her servant degenerates into a self-loathing presence that is the very last summation of a history of monarchic cruelty. There is a troubling voyeurism in reading the novel; we feel we are witness to something in the deep, dark, and diabolic history of our homeland we are not supposed to see.

The shadow of Golshiri's novella was still cast over the literary scene of the 1960s and 1970s, when Farmanara's masterful film adaptation of it, *Prince Ehtejab* (1974), extended its presence in visual terms.[12] The prose of the novella and the filmic diction of its adaptation both became aesthetically ahistorical and, as such, clairvoyant. In the opening sequence of the film, when Prince Ehtejab meets Morad, a former servant, in a dark alley, we witness a farewell to the world of archetypal monarchies and the history that had long abandoned them into the archival memories of nations. Today, it is no longer possible to distinguish between the novella and the film, as Golshiri himself was actively involved in production and co-wrote the script with Farmanara. The fusion of the novella and the film is the lasting legacy of a generation that lived under the Pahlavis and thought about the Qajars and what the entire history of monarchy has meant for them. The fusion of the two, and the censorial necessity of casting the critique of monarchy back to the one that was no longer in power, transformed contemporary Iranian history into the cataclysmic events of the Constitutional Revolution, when Iran as a nation parted ways with the very institution of monarchy.

In both the original novella and its cinematic adaptation, *Prince Ehtejab* is the story of a sustained course of moral decadence and political decline, a confusion and chaos at the heart of the Iranian encounter with colonial modernity, deeply rooted in its own archetypal legacies, when the creative and critical mind of the author faces the memories of the last Persian monarchy, before it yielded to a warlord named Reza Khan who wished to establish a new dynasty. The tragicomedy of the Pahlavi dynasty was precisely the project of building a belated monarchy when the nation it was meant to rule had evolved away from it. In my most recent book, *The Persian Prince: The Rise and Resurrection of an Imperial Archetype* (2023), I have detailed this archetype from its distant origins to its most recent gestations.[13] I frame my discussion of the Persian archetype following Machiavelli's iconic *The Prince* (1532) and the subsequent spin that the Italian Marxist thinker Antonio Gramsci put on it, before tracing the formation of the archetype in multiple cultural settings, from classical antiquity in Greece to the Hebrew Bible, to Indian and Iranian sources in their Arabic gestations. I built the archetype as a literary metaphor, a figurative authority and a persona that becomes operative in the context of successive Muslim and Iranian dynasties. My argument is to show how under colonial duress, beginning with the last three Muslim empires of the Ottomans, the Safavids, and the Mughals, the composition of the archetype begins to break down into its constituent forces and resurrects in the varied but interrelated figures of the poet, the prophet, the rebel, and ultimately the nomad. If we follow the logic of that argument, the figure of the Persian prince, and with it the institution of monarchy, have exhausted their historical potency and yielded to the compositional forces of these archetypes. The result is the social and political surfacing of far more potent and compelling revolutionary figures and subarchetypes; personae other than the character of the Persian prince himself.

What the militant Pahlavists lack in cultural depth, historical memory, and political persuasion, they compensate for with vociferous cyberspace propaganda, an outpouring of an avalanche of anger and obscenities unleashed toward anyone who dares to oppose or contradict them—evidently entirely unaware that the terror they have staged online is a premonition of how they will rule the nation should they come to power. The presence of the Pahlavi monarchists on the scene of the Zhina uprising, however, has one crucial consequence: it certifies the calamity of the Islamic Republic and its signature failure to convince a vast and deeply diversified nation of its legitimacy. The Islamic Republic is outdated, has smelled of mothballs for decades, and the rise of the Pahlavis at this moment in Iranian history is the clear indication that these two archetypal cornerstones of Iranian political culture—monarchy and mullarchy—have exhausted their legacies. In visual and performing arts, as well as in social sciences and humanities, and indeed in the collective memories of a nation, at large, the atrocities of an Islamic republic do not amount to a reversal of a reactionary history. They do not amount to a reversion to a monarchy that was defeated and dispensed with, especially when the leftovers of that monarchy have so completely wedded themselves to the most reactionary forces in American politics and consider a trip to the settler colony of Israel as their crowning achievement. The remnants of the Pahlavi sentiments have come back with a vengeance to the political scene, but the logic of Iranian history has moved far away from the gaudy relics of the monarchy and the Islamic Republic that supplanted it. Whatever was good and trustworthy in the figure of the Persian prince is now deconstructed back to its constituent forces in the figure of a poet, a prophet, a rebel, and a nomad. "Prince" Reza Pahlavi is none of those, so it's too little, too late. In the streets and squares of the country, young poets, with their defiant prophetic voices and rebellious uprisings, have become nomadic subjects on a plane of historical agency that is far removed from the tired old clichés of a decrepit mullah in Iran or a graceless ex-crown prince in the suburbs of Virginia. History moves forward.

EIGHT

TOWARD A POST-ISLAMIST LIBERATION THEOLOGY

The Executioner *(off-camera, his voice distorted):* *"What have you written in your last will and testament?"*

Majid Reza Rahnavard *(blindfolded, his hand hanging from an arm sling—nonchalantly):* *"Where to bury me. I don't like them to cry over my grave."*

The Executioner *(interrupting him):* *"You wrote that you wouldn't like anyone to recite the Quran for you or to perform a ritual prayer on you—what else?"*

Majid Reza Rahnavard: *"I don't want them to pray for me."*

The Executioner: *"I see."*

Majid Reza Rahnavard: *"I want them to be happy."*

The dialogue I cite above was the last exchange between masked executioners and Majid Reza Rahnavard (1999–2022), who was arrested, tortured, and, on December 12, 2022, at the age of twenty-three, publicly hanged because he had joined the protests against forty-three years of tyranny in the Islamic Republic. No sign of any regret from him, seemingly resigned to his fate, iconoclastic, publicly declining to have the ritual Muslim prayers recited for him when he was dead. Instead asking for his friends and family to be happy. The short exchange was abrupt, shocking, revealing, and defiant. In his evident rejection of Muslim rituals, there was a conviction of a different sort, a "theology" of a different gestation. One might even consider it a theology of liberation—liberation from hypocrisy, from cliché rituals, from the uses and abuses of Islam to justify almost half a century of brutal, juridically mandated dictatorship. The ruling regime is a republic of fear and loathing that the Shi'i clerical patriarchy established based on a brutish interpretation of Islamic law, subjecting millions of young and old people to their clerical whims, against their will. Majid Reza Rahnavard was boldly defiant of that violent jurisprudence, that jurisprudence of cruelty. There was something akin to the legendary moment when Mansour al-Hallaj (circa 858–922) was publicly executed, equally defiant, "I am the truth," he famously said as he walked toward the gallows. So did Majid Reza Rahnavard. The moment was mythic.

Now, listen to this music: it is called "Khoda Nur-e" (God is Light) and sung by Babak Amini and Ardavan Hatami.[1] The music video became widely popular during the Zhina uprising. Its lyrics are gut-wrenching, revelatory, and defiant. And yet the refrain is the word "God," or "Khoda" in Persian.

Khoda Nur-e,
Khoda Mahsast,
Khoda Soltan-e Qalb Nikast,
Khoda dar Kucheh hast Emruz
Shahamat dar vojud-e mast
Khoda Toumaj,

Khoda Saleh,
Khoda Emruz do ta baleh
Keh bayad par keshid ba oun—
Vagar nah ma'siat dareh—
Khoda zolfha-ye dar badeh—
Khoda Iran e abadeh

God is Light
God is Mahsa
God is the Sultan of Hearts Nika
God is in the streets today,
It is courage in our hearts
Khoda is Toumaj
Khoda is Saleh—God today are two wings
With which we must fly
Otherwise it'll be a sin—
God is the hair in the wind
God is the prosperous Iran[2]

All the names rhythmically and melodiously repeated in the lyric
are those of young Iranians murdered by the security and military
agents of the Islamic Republic in the course of the Zhina uprising: Khoda Nor Lojei, Mahsa Amini, Nika Shakarami, Toumaj
Salehi, and others. Eventually the song denounces the hypocrisy
of the ruling theocracy—and thus despite (or because of) its blas-
phemous diction, by the end of the song the singer has declared
a whole new "religion," or "faith," a whole new theology, or pantheology, a new way of imagining God, emphatic about a different
conception of divinity that lives in the enduring memories of every
murdered martyr. The song as a result reads like the roster of a new

martyrology. That religion, or faith, is no longer Islam, Christianity, or any other known religion, and yet it is not too far from the way a moral universe is imagined and yet betrayed in all such religions. The song imagines a moral universe, an ethical thrust about the world, and a sense of justice and fairness about life, and sings from the heart of that hope—in despair.

RETHINKING THEOLOGY

Let us briefly dwell on the moment of Majid Reza Rahnavard's execution. How could a man walking to his death be so certain of his refusal of the ritual ceremonies of his burial—thus making of his refusal a ritual of its own? Whence and wherefore that confidence—asking people not to pray but sing and be happy at his funeral? How have these words so calmly dismantled the entire edifice of the ruling theocracy systematically abusing a people's ancestral faith to torment them? There is a confidence about Majid Reza Rahnavard's wish, the assuredness with which he walks to his death, his belief that he has seen a truth beyond the reach of his executioners. No judge could ever judge him. He had reached his own judgment. The entire apparatus of the Islamic Republic had lost in that moment as had the entire contraption of disciplinary punishment of Islamic law. In the same vein: What is the word Khoda (God) doing in almost every phrase of Babak Amini and Ardavan Hatami's song? It reclaims a different gestation of God that emerges from the lived experiences of this generation, sick and tired of the ruling theocratic hypocrisy. On the surface this is blasphemy. God is not a fiction in the heavens, as the ruling clerics have portrayed the idea. God is on earth, and in those very fragile bodies that the agents of the Islamic Republic had murdered. The evident pantheism we hear in the song, mundane and material, is not odd at all. It is perfectly in line with the most sublime moments of Persian and Islamic mysticism, though in a provocative and contemporary way and straight out of the streets of Iran on fire, revolting against the ruling Islamic Republic, and its punishing Shariah having lost all legitimacy. Not just religion and piety and prayers but a whole new liberation theology is sung in this song with pitch-perfect harmony in the streets of a godforsaken homeland. In defiance of the ruling theocracy, the singer and songwriter are producing a new post-Islamist liberation theology—a theology of the real, of now, of the moment, of the fragilities of young boys and girls being murdered in cold blood.

That line of thinking raises another crucial question: How are we to think of the loaded binary opposition between "religion" and "secularism" after the moral demise of an Islamic Republic? How are we to think of it after a succession of uprisings in which not just the Islamic Republic but the very "Islam" that has given birth and legitimacy to it are categorically denounced? The ruling Islamist regime has a claim and is therefore denounced by its opposition as a "religious" regime, a theocracy, while the opposition declares its wishes to establish a solidly "secular" alternative. The very constitution of the Islamic Republic hinges on the idea of Velayat-e Faqih, the absolute authority and guardianship of a man who is well versed in Islamic law. People in Iran are fed up with the chimerical regime imposing "medieval" rules and regulations on them, or, even worse, imposing juridical mandates rooted in distant backward tribes that were canonized by and into Islamic law and are entirely inimical to a liberated and liberal life. This is the flawed and fearsome binary with which the ruling regime and its nemeses define the terms of their oppositions: one is religious and Islamic, the other is liberated and secular. What do we do with a word like "secular," for which we have no rooted word in Persian, Arabic, Urdu, Turkish? It is a neologism that has been force-fed to a language that has no use for it. "Secular" is like "the West." It is not a word; it is an ideology. In the same vein, every theology, *Kalam*, is also a pantheology, a reading of the indubitable in the midst of all doubts.

RELIGION VERSUS SECULARISM: THE FALSE BINARY

We might therefore look at the current moment through the two adjacent concepts of religion and the secular, as they have been perhaps most thoroughly questioned by anthropologist Talal Asad—and he did so from a solid critical position in the domain of capitalist modernity, which he diligently and persuasively historicized. In his *Genealogies of Religion* (1993), Asad correctly exposed "religion" as a European—Western, Christian—construct from which it was then colonially and therefore violently universalized, in effect as fodder for secularization-cum-subjugation of these societies. It was, therefore, a precursor to the colonially compromised modernity they had to undergo to become "civilized." From this configuration, Islam emerges as a defiantly political religion threatening the peace of the civilized, "secular" world. Anyone outside that secular modernity would be outside history, where the very idea of secularity becomes evident Christianity, where Christianity is secular as the secular becomes colonial. While for Foucault governmentality becomes Christian, and for Asad colonial, the combined forces of these two insights frame the modus operandi of understanding the binary of religion and secularity. Asad exposes the very idea of religion to be

the result of the European colonial conquest of defeated epistemologies, where a Hegelian teleology subjects the whole world to Christian eschatology. As Asad puts it from the outset:

> My anthropological explorations into Christian and
> post-Christian history are therefore motivated by the con-
> viction that its conceptual geology has profound implica-
> tions for the ways in which non-Western traditions are
> now able to grow and change. More particularly, I hold
> that anthropologists who would study, say, Muslim beliefs
> and practices will need some understanding of how "reli-
> gion" has come to be formed as concept and practice in
> the modern West. For while religion is integral to mod-
> ern Western history, there are dangers in employing it as a
> normalizing concept when translating Islamic traditions.[3]

The key issue here is the designation of the world at large, and its varied histories, in decidedly negational terms and as merely "non-Western," meaning the illusion of "the West" continues to operate as the
epistemological measure of the critique of, well, "Western modernity." In his dialogue with Marshall Sahlins, Asad makes a cogent
point about how people at the receiving end of capitalist modernity might be considered the authors of their own history.[4] Much
of Asad's concern is whether or not colonial subjects are capable of
autonomous thinking given the overwhelming epistemic power of
colonialism as a global system constituting terms such as "religion."
But underlying this assumption is not just the question of colonial
people being capable of resistance to colonialism while they have
access to the enormous resources of their own histories, cultures,
and civilizations before their brief and passing encounter with European colonial modernity. In his subsequent book, *Formations of the*

Secular (2003), Asad turns the table on the Orientalized oddity of
the idea of "religion" and offers secularity upheld as tantamount to
modernity, minus its extended colonial shadows, which he at least
implicitly identifies. Whereas secularity is the instrument of a new
governmentality, visible in and out of European self-universaliza-
tion, it actively seeks to conceal its own genealogical pedigree.

Now suppose we changed the location of our theorization away
from the self-delusional premise of "the West" to the lived realities of
Muslims themselves from, say, New York, where Asad did much of his
pioneering criticism of Tehran, where people are now up against an
Islamic republic and no one has the authority to question that official
and tyrannical claim to "Islam." In what ways does this "Islam" fit the
bill of the genealogies of religion, as Asad has articulated it? And in
what ways do the opposition's claims to a "secular" alternative meet
Asad's articulation of the formation of the secular? True, both the
ruling regime and its expat opposition are trapped inside the binary
that "Western modernity" has crafted for them—one religious and
the other secular. But what happens to the idea of "Islam" as a, well,
"religion," when it believes itself to be what its encounter with European colonial modernity thought and made it out to be? That is, a
"religion." Militant ideologues from Jamal al-Din al-Afghani to Ayatollah Khomeini to, perhaps most poignantly, Ali Shariati actively
made Islam what European colonial modernity made it out to be.
It perforce does to its adherents all the horrors that colonial modernity has thought Islam as a "religion" would—rob them of agency.
The genealogies Asad outlines, mostly in contestation with his fellow anthropologists, are domestic to European colonial modernity
and its critical interlocutors, falsely universalized by the power of
global capitalism, and now by a cogent anthropological critic of it.
That global capitalism generates resistance and defiance, however,

and does so not merely in reactive or reactionary ways, falls into the binary trap of religious and secular, the ruling Islamic Republic and its presumably "secular" opposition. The binary also assumes proactive and creative ways beyond the control of the current systems of colonial or postcolonial knowledge production. The entire ideological apparatus of the Islamic Republic, as I argued some thirty years ago in my *Theology of Discontent* (1993), is predicated on the illusion of "the West," as indeed the entire history of Islam was cast in dialogical terms against that very West.[5] Dismantling that binary, as I have done consistently for decades and more recently in my book *The End of Two Illusions* (2022), is both diagnostic and prognostic.

Here, Gil Anidjar's exposing the genealogy of the secular in Christianity is crucial:

> Christianity, then, actively disenchanted its own world by dividing itself into private and public, politics and economics, indeed, religious and secular. And Christianity turned against itself in a complex and ambivalent series of parallel movements, continuous gestures and rituals, reformist and counterreformist, or revolutionary and not so revolutionary upheavals and reversals while slowly coming to name that to which it ultimately claimed to oppose itself: religion. Munchausen-like, it attempted to liberate itself, to extricate itself from its own conditions; it judged itself no longer Christian, no longer religious. Christianity (that is, to clarify this one last time, Western Christendom) judged and named itself, it reincarnated itself as secular.[6]

In that sense, following both Asad's and Anidjar's arguments, and as I detailed it in *Theology of Discontent* (1993), the entire apparatus

of the Islamic ideology is a colonial construct built on the model
of a colonized conception of Islam, in which Muslim ideologues
were far more directly responsible than any European Orientalist
could ever be.

WHEN ISLAM SELF-COLONIZES

As "Christianity turned against itself," as Anidjar puts it, so did Islam
and Judaism—Islam into Islamism and Judaism into Zionism. The
Islam of the Islamic Republic has been self-colonizing, becoming
the medium through which Muslims are robbed of their own historical agency. The Islamic Republic has become the colonial extension
of what it has historically opposed. It continues to colonize a people, a culture, a humanity, as if on behalf of European colonialism.
As I have argued repeatedly, militant Islamism, political Zionism,
and Hindu fundamentalism are equally the by-products and the
extension of the very logic of European Christianity in the guise of
colonial modernity—modernizing the biopolitical technologies of
both statecraft and of governmentality. Muslims, in other words,
are doing to Muslims what European colonial modernity was once
doing to them. The idea that "religion" as the delusion of Christian
self-secularization has metamorphosed from militant totalitarianism to private domains spells out precisely the ideological formation
of the liberal capitalism that has historically enabled and privileged
very few and subjugated and disenfranchised the rest.

To ask the same seminal question in a slightly different way:
What happens to the idea of *the secular* when a Muslim society has
emerged from the hellhole of an Islamist theocracy of the most
vicious and abusive dimensions? Isn't it to shift ground from the

epistemic premise of "religion" to the emotive premise of the "secular"? If so, it would thus continue to operate within the occupied epistemologies of colonialism. Can we imagine a recasting of the secular and religion against the grain of their Christian imperial pedigree and into the domain of the temporal, of the worldly, of the historical? The idea of the secular became the kingpin of Christian modernity and therefore of colonialism. What happens, then, when the exposure to European colonialism becomes merely a passing phase in the long history of Muslim theologies and philosophies? What is now emerging from the collective consciousness of the societies thus brutalized by Islamist ideologies gives birth to newer and more potent pantheology beyond the reach of the terms *secular* or *religion*. The term post-Islamism, coined by Asef Bayat, has a latent liberation theology that has overcome the Islamist encounter with colonial modernity and reverted back to its historically dialogical disposition within its worldly contexts, as I detailed in *Being a Muslim in the World* (2013)[7] more than a decade ago. Being a Muslim in the world means a radical recasting of the very idea of Islam back onto its worldly character, categorically violated by Muslim ideologues themselves in the course of their frightful encounter with European colonialism, when the variegated fields of Islamic intellectual history were destroyed and leveled into a singular site of contestation against "the West." Liberated from a worn-out and discredited Shi'i clericalism, this post-Islamist theology is no longer at the disposal of the clerical class or any "religious intellectuals," as they call themselves, for should we overcome the false categories of secularity and religion, we face the fact that from Forough Farrokhzad's poetry, to Shirin Neshat's photography, to Abbas Kiarostami's cinema, to Shahrnoush Parsipour's fiction, and much more would all be at the disposal of a *liberation pantheism* rooted in Persian and the Islamic idea of *Vahdat al-Wujud* but irreducible to it, where being a Muslim in the world has thoroughly overcome and supplanted being a subject of Islamic law in its colonial gestations. This becomes a rooted liberation theology that transcends Islamic "pastoralism" through Mulla Sadra's *Transcendent Theosophy* (*al-Hikmat al-Muta'aliyah*). Here it is crucial to recall how Islamic law has never been the sole defining factor of Islam as such. It has always been morally, imaginatively, and epistemically questioned and challenged by Islamic philosophy and mysticism. All of those intellectual formations were socially and politically rooted, as is this post-Islamist liberation theology I propose here.

ISLAM AFTER THE WEST

That post-Islamist liberation theology is neither Islamic nor anti-Islamic, neither secular nor predicated on a Christian (colonial) conception of religion. Iran's experience over the last half century reverse engineers Talal Asad's ideas of religion, as he subjects it to a cogent anthropological scrutiny, as he does with the secular. Reverse-engineered, the collapse of the secular and religion becomes both the verification and the negation of Asad's assessment. It verifies, for the Islamic Republic has indeed acted as a militant Islam the way Asad said colonial modernity had made Islam believe itself to be under colonial duress, but also negates, because for half a century Islam was the primary agent of self-colonizing in potent and militant ways, so that Muslims became the corrosive force of colonizing their own critical judgemnts in ways that no Orientalist could ever do—until it exhausted that self-cannibalization. Ayatollah Khomeini and his lieutenants, going all the way back to Ali Shariati and before him to Jamal al-Din al-Afghani and Muhammad Abduh, were all agents of this potent self-colonization of Islam as a militant religion and as a result became the revolutionary mechanism of turning it into the secular—very much along the same lines that Zionism became the final stage of antisemitism. This fact preempts the claim of the opposition to the Islamist regime that they want to become secular, for the Islam of the Islamic Republic is the most secular, the most colonized, the most Christian of them all.

In *The End of Two Illusions* (2022) I articulated how the two fictional illusions of Islam and the West have been corrosive and have corroborated each other's mythic properties. This false, flawed, and colonially manufactured binary had to be broken down either between the two illusions or between the two terms they implicated: Islam was religious and the West secular. Just a year after the publication of my book, the Zhina uprising publicly dismantled that binary between religion and secularity. The post-Islamist liberation theology that is now emerging is the final delivery of "Islam and the West from the cul-de-sac into which they had trapped our contemporary history, and with it the colonially mitigated formations of 'religion' and 'the Secular.'" Liberated from that false binary, Islam once again becomes a floating signifier, restored to the agonistic pluralism that has historically defined and destined its being in the world. The Zhina uprising and the post-Islamist theology it has occasioned are the ground zero of that future unfolding of the inviolable in the violable, of the certain in the uncertainties to come.

IMAN AFTER ISLAM

What do we do in Persian (or Arabic or Turkish) when the word *din* (which is not "religion") has been abused to stand for religion? Suppose we cannot retrieve the *din* to stand for something other than religion. Then what? To avoid the conflation of religion and *din* we might turn to the word *iman* (faith) the way leading Iranian theologian, philosopher, and hermeneutician Mohammad Mojtahed Shabestari (born 1936) understands and places it next to the word *azadi* (freedom). In Shabestari's *Iman va Azadi* (Faith and Freedom, 1997), he opts for a word that is upstream from Islam and juxtaposes it with the word "freedom." His first move is to extract the word *iman* from the context of Islamic theologies, philosophies, and mysticism, and to consolidate the position of human agency in achieving a freedom-based *iman.*[8] From there he establishes the very definition of *iman* on the principle of the freedom of inquiry and agency in choice. He completely separates the idea of *iman* from any social setting or political consideration and takes it as a hermeneutic principle predicated on freedom of human agency. In a not-so-subtle reference to the ruling Islamist regime, he severely criticizes political abuses of faith in the name of *iman.* In *iman,* a person has reached individuality, he suggests in a profoundly Kierkegaardian move, and this person is the *ensan-e beh fardiyyat rasideh* (the human who has reached individuality),[9] which is ultimately predicated on freedom.[10] Islam in this choice becomes secondary to *iman,* for *iman* is the result of freedom of inquiry that includes consideration of Islam but is not limited to it.

If we were to believe in that freedom as the sine qua non of *iman,* then the post-Islamist liberation theology I have thought through for some time now will have to go back and critically reexamine the idea of secularity. There and then we see a pantheon of poets like Forough

Farrokhzad, Mehdi Akhavan-e Sales, Ahmad Shamlou, and Sohrab Sepehri who are waiting, with the most spectacular art movement of the mid-twentieth century, the Saqqa-khaneh moment, as its potent aesthetic manifestation. Farrokhzad's iconic poem, "Kasi keh Mesl-e Hich Kas Nist" (Someone Who Is Like No One); Shamlou's equally important poems "Ebrahim dar Atash" (Abraham in Fire) and "Marg-e Naseri" (the Death of the Nazarene); as well as the centrality of the figure of Zarathustra in Akhavan-e Sales's poetry gave the movement a particularly potent prophetic dimension. Add to that selective list Sepehri's sublime stanza, "I am a Muslim," in his iconic poem "The Sound of the Footstep of Water," and you have a pantheology that crosses over all the so-called Abrahamic religions without yielding to any one of them. *Iman*, to go back to Shabestari's idea, was present at the heart of the contemporary Iranian poetic imagination, but Shabestari was looking for it in the wrong places. As a Muslim theologian, he was not conversant, or at least we have no public record of it, with the Persian poetic imagination of his own time. Consider this excerpt from Shamlou's "Marg-e Naseri" (the Death of the Nazarene, 1965), which was composed in memorial celebration of the moment of Jesus's crucifixion.

Ba Avazi yek-dast . . .

With a monotonous song
Monotonous,
The tail end of the wooden load
Drew a heavy and shivering line
Behind him—
Upon the earth.

"Put a crown of thorns on his head!"

As the long song
Of the load behind him—
In the hallucinations of his pain—
Wove a fiery thread.

"Hurry up, Nazarene, hurry up!

He felt light
From the forgiveness he found in his own soul
And like a proud swan
He gazed upon his own purity.

"Whip him!" . . .

"Hurry up, Nazarene, hurry up! . . .
The overcast heavens
Heavily
Lowered upon the silencing song of forgiveness—
The mourners
Climbed the mount:
And the sun and the moon embraced.[11]

The overwhelming presence of Christian and Jewish imagery in Persian poetry, past and present, is not unusual. But here in Shamlou's poem his Christianity is substitutional, not just for his lapsed Islam but for any other form of piety, as his poetic diction borrows from the Christian iconography to recast the meaning of *iman* in a language that is neither Islamic nor Christian but entirely poetic.

The images of Jesus or Abraham remain constant in Shamlou's poetry as revolutionary figures to whom he approximated his contemporary heroes, for whom he composed most of these poems. Toward the end of my book on Jalal Al-e Ahmad, *The Last Muslim Intellectual* (2020), I began thinking through the idea of a post-Islamist liberation theology and how it might look in a post-democratic world. I have been preoccupied with this idea and the idea of alterity instead of identity since I wrote *Islamic Liberation Theology: Resisting the Empire* (2008). Today, post-Islamist theology must move away from the ruling dualism of Islam and the West and the entire history of Islam of the last two hundred years and recast the faith in a postcolonial world where Islam and the West are no longer a valid binary. If we did so, the succession of these uprisings are the clearest indications that the history of that duality has come to an end. We must abandon and overcome the religious/secular binary and reclaim them both in a post-Islamist pantheology that generates and sustains its own metaphysics of alterity. The false religious/secular binary was forcefully superimposed on the world. If we shift from Islam to *iman*, as Shabestari does, the Islamic Republic can collapse and with it the Islam of the last two hundred years that was manufactured in opposition to the illusion of the West. But the post-Islamist world that will follow will have already found its lived realities in the poetries of Shamlou, Farrokhzad, Sales, Sepehri, and in the Saqqa-khaneh artistic movement, where we search for a vision of the invisible and the certainty that sustains the dialectics of all unfolding uncertainties.

CONCLUSION

CAN THE SUBALTERN SPEAK PERSIAN?

Nah misheh ba kasi sohbat koni
Na royato ba kasi qesmat koni . . .

You can't talk to anyone here—
You can't share your dreams with anyone—
You can't be kind to anyone here—You'll catch my drift if
*   you just pay close attention to what I say—*
I don't want to change at all—
I don't want to get into trouble or get anyone else into
*   trouble—*
For whatever I did I was humiliated—
Am just thirteen years old—
How soon I became old!
Let me be frank with you—
Tell you like it is—why should I be coy bro?
Everyone climbs over our back—
They'd have fun with it and at the end they'd just curse us!
If you hear someone badmouthing us— Don't take it too
*   seriously—*

Just tell them ok fine whatever you say—
Constant bickering and constant fights—
At the end nothing happens at all—
Love is entirely tasteless here—
If you're humble they'd crush you under their feet—

Constant bickering and constant fights—
At the end nothing happens at all—
Love is entirely tasteless here—
If you're humble they'd crush you under their feet.

—**Arya Akbari**, age thirteen (2022)

Back in January 2018, before the Zhina uprising commenced in September 2022, on the occasion of yet another massive revolt against the ruling Islamist theocracy, I published an essay seeking to explain to my readers what was happening in Iran. "In the most widespread series of demonstrations in Iran against structural poverty, rampant corruption, and political tyranny in almost a decade," I wrote, "mostly poor, underemployed, and unemployed Iranians poured into the streets of their country and challenged the ruling apparatus of the Islamic Republic."[1] As I conclude this book on the Zhina uprising, I find it necessary to stress how much of the writing I have shared with my readers over the last four decades echoes the same line of thinking: the Islamic Republic is dysfunctional, and a politically significant portion of Iranian population has consistently and systematically poured into the streets to make this fact known. These periodic uprisings are not incidental but definitive to the troubled course of this

Islamic Republic ever since its very inception in the aftermath of the 1977 to 1979 revolution.

In that January 2018 essay, as indeed in this book, my concern remains how to read these recurrent uprisings. What do they mean? I continued in that essay to talk about the economic roots and social consequences of the revolt. The ruling regime was habitually dismissing the uprising as instigated by foreigners, while the Trump administration sought in vain to assume the higher moral ground by denouncing the crackdown (which was quite rich coming from perhaps the most corrupt US administration in recent memory). The question I raised in that essay remains valid today: "How do we know what we know and say about these or any other such protest movements—from the Green Movement to the Arab Spring, and now down to these nameless uprisings in Iran?" I responded by detailing the facts on the ground: "An incompetent, self-righteous, ideologically blinded conservative leadership; an even more incompetent and corrupt reformist camp; a small class of obscenely wealthy nouveau riche and their brazenly conspicuous consumption; rampant unemployment and underemployment; an angry and hateful generation facing an economic dead end. These provide for combustible circumstances, however you look at it."

Referencing Spivak's seminal 1988 essay "Can the Subaltern Speak?"[2] and the linguistic differential between the events and the way people read them, I concluded: "As a political subject, the subaltern is therefore conditioned for indexical expressions only it understands, unable (and perhaps even unwilling) to reach the layered hegemonies of the states and empires that rule over its destiny. The subaltern is the walking embodiment of a power differential—in language and truth, fact and theory—that can never be trespassed." My conclusion was simple:

> In its intents, contentions, and interpretations, the most
> eloquent language the Iranians spoke in these rallies
> beyond any shadow of doubt is when they smashed win-
> dows and set buildings on fire. There was no misreading,
> no misinterpreting, no false exegesis here. The subaltern
> in Iran, in the Arab and Muslim world, or else in Asia,
> Africa, or Latin America does not speak English. Like all
> the subalterns around the globe, they speak in the lan-
> guage of their angered frustrations, of their constitutional
> alienation from any language that seeks to understand,
> analyze, interpret, and pacify their sufferings. The most
> eloquent language that they can speak is therefore when
> they are burning a building down, or when they leave their
> broken and dead bodies on the front line that separates
> their sufferings from the question: Can the subaltern
> speak . . . English?[3]

The question today is whether there is any other diction left that a nation can use to speak its pains and seek remedy other than the language of suffering and defiance and violence. Periodically we witness these revolts and give them a name like the Green Move-ment, the Zhina uprising, or, when the Reform Movement started, the Second Khordad. The ruling regime, beginning with Supreme Leader Ali Khamenei, denounces and dismisses them all as a plot by the everlasting "enemy." The leading global media pay passing attention to them, the expats get excited, and some of their worst career opportunists seek to bank on them and cash out, and then things quiet down and eventually become distant memories. In my view, there is no need to over-interpret what these uprisings mean, and there is one lesson to be learned from them all: the nation and the state are two incongruent ideas, things, entities, propositions. Those proverbial apples and oranges. They don't mesh, they don't gel, they don't belong to each other. It is a false binary. Once and for all we need to let them go their separate ways. I believe this to be the case anywhere in the world, but most particularly I believe this to be the case for postcolonial nations and their painful and useless experiments with the colonial concoction of the nation-state. This conclusion is not by way of any sophisticated political theory. It is the sum total of our lived experiences. We will simply never have a state that will be the representative of the democratic will of the nation.

Now, where do we go from here?

NOT A TOTAL REVOLUTION, BUT A SUCCESSION OF INTIFADAS

I have argued here and elsewhere that the Arab revolutions of 2009 to 2010 and, even before them, the Green Movement of 2008 to 2009 were not total revolutions but open-ended revolutions, or else delayed or deferred defiance. Following this line of thought, we might see the history of Iran's encounter with colonial modernity, from the Tobacco Revolt of 1890 against British colonialism to the present, as one long pattern of uprisings, a pattern of revolutionary resurrection and interruptions, followed by other resumptions and interruptions.[4] We might also view this succession of uprisings as the pattern of the Hegelian Geist unfolding, not toward the ideal formation of the state but toward the fulfillment of the prospect of the nation, not multiple subnations, as the opportunist ethnic separatists might claim, but one nation formed pluralistically—or perhaps more accurately in agonistic pluralism—from the ruins of former empires and in the crucible of the colonial encounter with European modernity as the optimum modus operandi of the will to resist power. Today there are Arab separatists in southern Iran who wish to call Khuzestan Arabestan, and to call Ahvaz Ahwaz, and take the Khuzestan oil wells and rush to become a sheikhdom like Qatar, Bahrain, Kuwait, or the United Arab Emirates. There are indeed some Turks or Kurds who wish to part ways with the rest of Iran and rush into some other ethnic collectivity, all of them overriding the lived experiences of successive polities in which all Iranians from the four corners of their homeland have been engaged. No one can blame a Kurd, a Turk, a Baluch, or an Arab citing relentless discriminations and brutalities of the centralizing states denying them their pride of place. But ethnic nationalism and the formation of an ethnic state is the saddest resolution to that tragic history. Partition of the entirety of the pluralistic nation from the state is where the lived experiences of Iranians over the last two centuries result not in multiple ethnic states, one more miserably undemocratic than the other, but a pluralistic nation against any centralizing state.

Today the totality of the postcolonial nation posits antagonistic attitudes toward the very idea of the state. That fact is rooted in the long and arduous history of the two entities—the multifaceted nation going one way and the centralizing tyranny of the state the other way. From the Russo-Persian wars of the early nineteenth century, the moral imagination of the nation was formed against the sustained incompetence of the Qajar dynasty. The Babi movement of the 1840s was the most powerful mobilization of the revolutionary potential of the nation against the Qajar dynasty. The movement was later consolidated in the Tobacco Revolt of 1890 and came to full political fruition in the course of the Constitutional Revolution of 1906 to 1911. The rise of Reza Shah in the 1920s seized upon the colonial need of a centralizing state to control the unleashed power of the multifaceted nation and its socialist proclivities, while the 1941 Anglo-Soviet invasion and occupation of Iran rekindled that anticolonial nationalism, which ultimately resulted in the abdication of Reza Shah and the succession of his son Mohammad Reza Shah to form the next totalizing, centralizing state on behalf of the selfsame colonial interests—a balancing act between the Russian and the British interests first and the Soviets and Americans next. The establishment of the Tudeh Party in 1949 marked the formation of the first potent political party that yielded to Soviet supremacy rather than aiding in the fate of the rising nation—for which reason the party was soon dismantled and discredited as its leaders ran away to Eastern Europe and the Soviet Union. The failed assassination of Mohammad Reza Shah in 1949 eventually led to the anticolonial nationalism of Mohammad Mosaddegh and the nationalization of the Iranian oil industry, which resulted in the CIA-MI6 coup of 1953 and soon after that the 1963 Khomeini uprising, when an Islamist take on the nation digested its ideological nemeses and put them to effective political use. All along the way the domestic reactionary forces from the inside and the colonial forces from the outside have insisted on consolidating this state as the nation becomes more multifaceted and defiant—with the separatist movements a symptom of this forced binary of the whole nation and the totalizing state. In 1965 after the second assassination attempt against the Shah, the ruling regime consolidated state power, while the February 1971 Siahkal uprising put a defiant Marxist revolutionary claim on the nation. By now the revolutionary disposition of the nation and its periodic revolts against the ruling state had become second nature to it, written into its political DNA, as it were.

The 1977 to 1979 Iranian Revolution brought the nationalist, Islamist, and Marxist forces together and toppled the Shah, while the 1979 to 1981 hostage crisis and the 1980 to 1988 Iran-Iraq War consolidated the rule of the Islamist state over the revolutionary nation. During the 1985 to 1987 Iran-Contra affair, the duplicitous opportunism of the Islamist regime was exposed, while the 1988 Salman Rushdie affair created yet another smoke screen under which the Islamists further institutionalized their state power. It was during the 1997 Reform Movement that the nation sought to reclaim the power of the state and weaken the ruling regime, which, when that failed, resulted in the 1999 student protests. By 2009 the Green Movement posited the most serious challenge to the ruling state. The movement was brutally suppressed before it resurfaced during the 2017 widespread protests, which again turned out to be a dress rehearsal for the 2022 Mahsa (Zhina) Amini uprising. None of the momentous uprisings in Iran—Khizesh, as I have called them, on the model of Intifada—are in isolation from the others. These revolts form a chain reaction to state tyranny and as such are the rhyme and rhythm, the pulse and pace, of the restless, defiant, and determined nation. The result: total and final discrediting of any and all ruling states ever having any legitimate claims over this historically self-conscious, enabled and empowered nation.

THE NEXT REVOLUTION WILL NOT BE THEORIZED

This is the historical premise on which I propose the next Iranian revolution will not be (for it cannot be) theorized, or televised, for all national uprisings in a post-democratic world have now entered a phase of total historical meltdown. The uprising we now know as Zhina has global implications in the sense that it is the first social revolt in the context of post-democratic history when major European philosophers and our own lived experiences have collectively declared (in two different but complimentary senses) the final demise of democracy as a project. This movement is also in the context of the rise of proto-fascist politics in Europe, India, Brazil, and the United States, to which must be added the institutional defeat of the Arab revolutions. Put in the Iranian context, it has its own momentum in this historical moment—"Make Iran Great Again" or even "Make Persia Great Again," straight from the streets of Los Angeles in support of both Trump and the Pahlavis, with the late Shah appearing in posters wearing the red MAGA hat—a carnival full of the most grotesque imageries that mark where the fascistic sentiments of pro-Pahlavi zealots rise. From the grassroots revolts in Zahedan and Kurdistan to these ludicrous carnivals of expat monarchists in California and Washington, DC, the pulse of the nation casts any political uprising in decidedly post-democratic terms. That hidden dialectic could be neither the subject of learned doctoral dissertations nor the sound bites of a television infomercial, nor indeed would it fit the limited characters that you could tweet around cyberspace. The pace of the revolutionary uprising in a post-democratic world is atonal.

What, then, is this Zhina uprising? It is at its roots a total rejection of the idea of a totalizing state, the Islamists and all its alternates, without a vision of a state to replace it. It is the first revolutionary uprising (not a "revolution" in the classical sense of the term, but "revolutionary" in its decidedly subversive urges—and therefore always just a Khizesh) without a vision of what it is to succeed the status quo. This is perhaps its political weakness but also its revolutionary strength. There is, of course, the Reformist front of various shades inside Iran, the cult of MEK, and the proto-fascist force behind the Pahlavi legacy—but precisely because they are so self-contained and insular there is no compromise among them, for which reason looms the final breakdown of the nation-state. The Zhina uprising reflects a radical reshaping and restructuring of an unruly public sphere and a recasting of the student, labor, and women's organized formations. Therefore, not any totalizing state but a confederation of voluntary associations based on gender, class, and common economic struggles remains the only institutional salvation of this country. Beyond that looms the blind hatred of the state, for all the right and wrong reasons, and the plots of the cultic MEK and the fascist Pahlavi legacy to compete with the ruling Islamist tyranny.

Iranian women, to paraphrase the proverbial saying, do not need saving, but their lived experiences of the last two hundred years have also liberated them from the cliché conceptions of what a "Muslim woman" should look like. Islam is integral to their lives but not definitive to it. They have once and for all proved Fanon wrong: they can come out of their veils, challenge domestic tyranny and foreign domination alike, and redefine what it means to be an Iranian, a Muslim, and a worldly woman. They need not veil (in a cliché and patriarchally mandated law) to prove they are defiant against colonialism. One can veil and defy patriarchy. One can unveil and accommodate tyranny. Boldly questioning what it means to be a worldly woman and thus a man, they have also unpacked the patriarchal constitution of binary gender formations and created a social space for the LGBTQ+ communities. The genealogies of the "secular" and perforce of "religion" have

also passed their theorization from the bosom of European colonial discourse. Iran's case recasts the terms of the argument, not
against veiling as a token of being religious, but being pro-choice in
a vastly different and worldly disposition of being a person. Iranian
women have exposed the lie hidden in the nexus between "Islam
and the West," which has paradoxically been consolidated and
exacerbated in the reception of the critical work of Edward Said
and Talal Asad. The fate of anticolonial discourse, from Fanon to
Said to Asad has become a normative and reactive critique. We
need to be proactive, for this is where being reactive becomes reactionary, and the critique of the West from the bosom of the West,
becomes, well, Western, and into which Muslims are trapped.
This uprising in Iran is the first feminist movement by women, as
Muslims and non-Muslims at one and the same time—while the
bourgeois feminism of characters like Nazanin Boniadi, Masih
Alinejad, and Golshifteh Farahani perpetuate the commodified
fetish impersonated in the "secular" post-Muslim person. These
slow-motion subterranean forces could not possibly be televised or
tweeted. Civilized people need civilized discourses, composed in
sentences with multiple subordinate clauses.

Commodity fetishism of body politics of the most reactionary sort consolidates retrograde Islamophobia as feminism. The
strong signs of fascism, of commodification of revolt, and a sense
of Islamophobia mark the white supremacy and xenophobia evident in the Zhina uprising. The problem that most progressives,
especially Arab and Muslim progressives, have with the Iranian
uprisings (from the Reformist Movement to the Green Movement to the Zhina uprising) is not political but epistemic. They
don't know how to read these movements, which are integral to
all other revolutionary uprisings in their neighborhood but also

something quite specific, and that specificity is not theorized, the way generations of Palestinians or African Americans have theorized themselves. We therefore have a revolutionary momentum in Iran; its internal idiomaticness is yet to be made decipherable to its regional and global readership. My work of the last few decades has been primarily dedicated to this task. That theorization is inimical to the substance and the logic of these uprisings being broken down to television sound bites or Instagram stories.

THE MIXED BLESSINGS
OF EXPAT REVOLUTIONARIES

The delusional dream of a total revolution and the imminent collapse of the Islamist regime is driven by an expat cacophony of keyboard revolutionaries, weekend activists either on pension in Europe or else retirement in the United States, and their rich and successful or else unemployed offspring, all under the thin veneer of a liminality made possible by the fancy footwork of the internet, both hyperreal and unreal. After two hundred years of repeated attempts at achieving democracy and jumping from the ditch of a tyrannical monarchy into the hellhole of a fanatical theocracy, this nation is done trying. The deep-rooted frustration has assumed a nostalgic resignation that fosters the most bitter revolutionary disposition of a radical defiance of false promises. This is neither a case of classical anarchy nor a resorting to passive mysticism. Quite the contrary. This is the most robust, alert, life-affirming, and beautiful revolutionary act that has successfully sublated the historic experiences of a nation into a political stance that no democratic promise can ever pretend to deliver. Led by women, the doubly tyrannized by all ruling regimes, Iranians are finally delivered from any and all false promises and have suspended all self-deceptive hopes of achieving a democratic state. They are neither sad nor resigned but delivered to a far richer and more enabling liberation from false promises. A military coup by the Pasdaran, or else a military strike by the United States and Israel, may indeed topple this regime, but nothing will change in the actual political imagination of the liberated nation, as it will never succumb to the false promises of the ruling regime or its adversaries. Sporting its monopoly of violence, the ruling state and its nemeses have gone one way and the richly multifaceted nation the other way. No other state can ever fool or rule this nation.

Iran is now emerging as the first postcolonial nation openly and happily declaring itself liberated from the headache and heartache of the postcolonial state that, since the Qajar dynasty of the early nineteenth century, has been the source of nothing but calamity for the nation and indignity for any decent human being who has called themselves "Iranian." Neither the endemic corruption and incompetence of the Qajars, nor the wasted oil-boomed hubris of the Pahlavis, nor the fanatical clericalism of the Islamist theocracy could have offered a modicum of democratic pride of place to a single Iranian. Today the separatists in Kurdistan, Azerbaijan, Baluchistan, or Khuzestan have every reason not to want anything to do with a ruling central state. Their calamity, however, is that they may think, with their version of bourgeois ethnic nationalism, that they will end up with a better state than the one they wish to leave. This is delusional. Sectarian nationalism is made of the same cloth as the ruling regimes they justly denounce. The issue is no longer leaving one state and forming another but disbanding the very idea of state altogether.

All the vacuous promises of democratic delivery—from the reactionary monarchists to the weakened and dispirited left, from the discredited reformists to the treacherous MEK—targeting a recalcitrant and deeply corrupt garrison state—are either pure acts of charlatanism or else entirely delusional. My core political solidarity has always been and remains with the progressive and self-critical left. But I see no demographic, institutional, or ideological formations that will give the left a chance to overthrow this garrison state and withstand a free and fair chance at a democratic state. Even more importantly, the very idea of state—revolutionary or reactionary—has lost its raison d'être in Iran. All states are founded on force, as Max Weber cited Leon Trotsky as having said at Brest-Litovsk in 1918 and rightly so. To triumph over its entrenched enemies on its right or liberal sides, the left will have to resort to armed struggles and therefore a violence even worse than that wielded by the ruling regime, and that would be far removed from any legitimate claim to a democratic state. All these forces, from the left of the left to the right of the right, must have fair and transparent access to democratic process—which today is an impossibility. Ultimately the answer to securing any semblance of democracy in the future is in voluntary associations of labor, students, and women to mobilize and resist all tendencies of the totalizing states, left or right.

Democracy has never been but an empty and circuitous metaphor at the colonial edges of its European assumptions and rhetoric. This impossibility began with European colonialism putting a gun to our head and telling us to be free—and to this day Europeans have not noted the irony. Not a single postcolonial state around the globe has anything remotely resembling a living democratic organicity. Democracy was not meant for us. India has always had a dubious claim to being the largest democracy in the world, and today two pages into reading any book by Arundhati Roy, you realize Indian democracy is a joke.[5] A Hindu fanaticism of the most pernicious sort that has gone into battle with the pluralistic disposition of India severely afflicts that claim. The same is true for the so-called oldest democracy in the world: the chickens of the violent coups the United States has staged around the globe have now come home to roost in its streets and in the citadels of its democratic institutions. Europe is plagued by the most patently fascistic traits in its daily politics. From Mexico to Argentina to Brazil, we see no democratic model either. The entire landscape of the colonial space carved and called "the Middle East" is now under the extended shadow of Israel, the last European colonial garrison state making a mockery of the very idea of democracy.

If, based on our historical experiences, democracy is not attainable to us anytime soon, if ever, then what are these uprisings for? Democracy for postcolonial societies is an ideological battleground for various forces to flex their muscles and spread themselves out. The cast of characters I have mentioned in this work, from the ruling theocracy and its praetorian guards, to the monarchists who wish to pull the country back to the status quo ante of the ancien régime, to the outdated and reactionary cult of MEK, to career opportunist regime changers, to an assortment of leftist sentiments with no organizational infrastructure to give them meaningful political momentum—these characters will not bring about any pending democracy. They either exacerbate the ruling tyranny or seek to succeed it with worse consequences.

The healthy and robust exchanges that have historically existed between progressive forces inside Iran and the expat communities outside have lost all their organic momentum and yielded to barbaric backbiting and corrupt allegiances to nondemocratic forces. The most caring and competent Iranian thinkers and scholars write their serious work in English, French, or German, and even if translated into Persian their work is entirely marginalized and ineffective, while the most career opportunist charlatans tweet their gibberish in Persian and work for reactionary outfits like the Washington Institute for Near East Policy in Washington, DC, or the Hoover Institution in California, covering the political spectrum from one end of retrograde US politics to the next. Gone is the era when a handful of expat intellectuals in Delhi, Calcutta, Cairo, Istanbul, Berlin, Paris, or London revolutionized the political culture of their homeland, writing all their iconoclastic tracts in Persian and disseminating them widely inside Iran. There is very little promise and much peril to the expat Iranians who have increasingly looked and acted like reactionary Cubans collaborating with racist outfits in US politics.

THE POTENT ILLUSION OF DEMOCRACY

There is a potent use, however, to the illusion of democracy, which must remain the level playing field among all these factions, all of them the result of the postcolonial condition of the impossibility of democracy. The European and American philosophers reflecting on the continued prospects of democracy are ultimately operating within a vacuum with little to no significance or relevance for the rest of the world. When they ask if it is meaningful to call oneself a democrat, and, if so, how do you interpret the word, they do so entirely oblivious to the colonial terror their "Europe" has perpetrated upon the globe and trapped within the limited hermeneutic horizons of the history of European political thought.[6] The idea of democracy still remains potent and productive for them precisely in face of the compelling prospects of fascism of their past and perhaps even future, but in a globally blinded environment. Speaking of "constitutions" and "democratic communism" when the settler colony of Israel is the crowning achievement of their brutal political practices, about which all European states aggressively and actively concur on "the gift" they have left behind when they packed their colonial flags and left, is a little too heavy with irony. The sustained history of their antisemitism, culminating in the Jewish Holocaust, and their common consensus that Palestinians must pay for their thoroughly European crimes against humanity is what the world hears when reading European philosophers who reflect on "democracy."

Between the violent neoliberal and neoconservative movements using the idea as a rallying flag to invade, occupy, and dismember countries, the very idea of democracy has a shaky premise to global credulity. The issues of these European philosophers preoccupied with democracy remains how to define "the left" after the demise of Soviet Union! This is decidedly not our issue. Soviet communism for us amounted to yet another form of European or Eurasian imperialism. We on the postcolonial edges of European modernity have no choice but to begin with the fact that the European conception of the nation-state has wreaked havoc in our lives. But the fact is that both reactionary theocracies and the prospects of fascist monarchies (both homegrown) have ancient archetypes they invoke and operationalize. We who wish for a better future do not have any such readily available archetypes and must seek to turn those we have received upside down. Our archetypes are the defiant poets as the prophetic figures who are the harbingers

of smashing their false gods. Without them we become mere spec-
tators to the continued European games played by our monarchs
and mullahs. If the "deliberative democracy" of which leading
European philosophers like Jürgen Habermas were advocating is
limited in its global imagination, then could the "agonistic pluralism" of the sort Chantal Mouffe is advocating be more embracing?[7]
Perhaps. Mouffe's idea of agonistic pluralism seeks to correct the
course of deliberative democracy by pointing out that it actually does not embrace pluralism but subjects it to an ideological
hegemony. This sounds perfectly true to a set of colonial ears. The
agnostic pluralism she articulates seeks to enable that pluralism
and strives to sustain "a conflictual consensus." Beyond European
solutions to global problems they have created in the first place,
still in the same spirit of conflictual consensus, democracy for
us can only remain an enabling myth and a working trope, not a
solution, more a battlefield than a resting place. Independent labor
unions, I repeat and rest my case, nationwide student assemblies,
and above all women's rights organizations: these are our only salvation, the way forward to demand and exact, not to promise and
fail to deliver, our fair and just share in this world.

ACKNOWLEDGMENTS

I am grateful to Anthony Arnove and Brekhna Aftab of Haymarket for their gracious support and endorsement of my book. The inimitable Brekhna Aftab gave my manuscript a detailed, probing, and deeply insightful read and gave me copious notes for revisions, which I gratefully accepted. She is a blessing to have as an editor. My research assistant Rukhsar Balkhi was prompt and punctual in her work during the final stages of preparing my book for production. I am grateful to Al Jazeera and *Middle East Eye* for their kind permissions to use parts of my previous writings in this volume. I thank the editors of World Literature Today for their kind permission to cite the English translation of the Kurdish poet Sherko Bekas's "Answer" (1988). Ramin Bahrani, Foad Torshizi, Atefeh Akbari, Firoozeh Kashan-Sabet, Ali Mirsepassi, Akbar Ganji, Peyman Vahabzadeh, Moises Garduño Garcia, Mahfarid Mansourian, Marziyeh Vafamehr, and Karim Malak were my most immediate and trusted interlocutors during the time I was writing this book. I am grateful to them and cherish their friendship and comradery. I dedicate this book to Farhad Arshad, in gratitude of his decades of steady and unwavering friendship.

PERMISSIONS

Portions of "Revolutionary Aspirations in a Post-Democratic World"
first appeared in "Women, Life, Freedom: How Iran Protests Were
Foretold in Film," *Middle East Eye*, December 16, 2022, https://
www.middleeasteye.net/opinion/iran-protests-women-life-free-
dom-film-foretold-how.

"The Real Perils and the False Promises of Ethnic Nationalism"
includes writing first published as "On the Kurdish Question," Al
Jazeera, November 27, 2017, https://www.aljazeera.com/opin-
ions/2017/11/27/on-the-kurdish-question.

"Can the Subaltern Speak Persian?" was first published as "Can the
Subaltern Speak English?" Al Jazeera, January 18, 2018, https://
www.aljazeera.com/opinions/2018/1/18/can-the-subaltern-speak-
english.

The poem "Answer" (1988), by Sherko Bekas and translated by Alana
Marie Levinson-LaBrosse and Halo Fariq, was first published in
World Literature Today, July 2018.

NOTES

INTRODUCTION: WHAT IF "DEMOCRACY" WAS IN BAD FAITH?

Alain Badiou, "The Democratic Emblem," in *Democracy in What State?*, Giorgio Agamben et al., eds. (New York: Columbia University Press, 2011), 6–7.

1. Giorgio Agamben et al., eds. *Democracy in What State?* (New York: Columbia University Press, 2011).
2. Hannah Arendt, *On Revolution* (London: Penguin, 1963/1990), 255.
3. Ali Mirsepassi, *Iran's Quiet Revolution: The Downfall of the Pahlavi State* (Cambridge: Cambridge University Press, 2019).
4. Asef Bayat, *Revolution without Revolutionaries: Making Sense of the Arab Spring* (Stanford, CA: Stanford University Press, 2017).
5. ACLU, "The Global Suppression of Protest," October 10, 2013, https://www.aclu.org/news/national-security/global-suppression-protest.
6. Radley Balko, *Rise of the Warrior Cop* (New York: Public Affairs, 2014).
7. Edith Garwood, "With Whom Are Many US Police Departments Training? With a Chronic Human Rights Violator - Israel," Amnesty International, August 25, 2016, https://www.amnestyusa.org/with-whom-are-many-u-s-police-departments-training-with-a-chronic-human-rights-violator-israel/.

ONE: REVOLUTIONARY ASPIRATIONS IN A POST-DEMOCRATIC WORLD

Mohammad Haqmoradi, "The Zhina Event and the Non-Ideology of Women, Life, Freedom," *Naqd-e Eqtesad-e Siasi*, November 2022, https://pecritique.com/2022/11/28/رخ‌داد-ژینا-و-ناایدئولوژی-زن،-زندگی-آ. Translation from the Persian original is mine.

1. Saman Safarza'i, "Sargijeh-ye Enqelabi-ye Asef Bayat" (The Revolutionary Confusion of Asef Bayat), Shargh Daily, https://www.sharghdaily.com/روزنامه-142778/001-سرگیجه-انقلابی-آصف-بیات/خش.

217

2. See Bayat, *Revolution without Revolutionaries*.
3. Asef Bayat, *Life as Politics: How Ordinary People Change the Middle East* (Stanford, CA: Stanford University Press, 2010), 16.
4. Haqmoradi, "The Zhina Event."
5. Haqmoradi, "The Zhina Event."
6. See Wendy Brown, "We Are All Democrats Now," in *Democracy in What State?*, Giorgio Agamben et al., eds. (New York: Columbia University Press, 2011), 44–57.
7. Brown, "We Are All Democrats," 44.
8. Brown, "We Are All Democrats," 44.
9. Brown, "We Are All Democrats," 46.
10. Brown, "We Are All Democrats," 54–55.
11. The letter was widely published and circulated in Persian venues. See Iran Wire, "Bahareh Hedayat from Evin Prison: Revolution Is Certain," December 22, 2022, https://iranwire.com/fa/news-اختصاصی-بهاره-هدایت-از-زندان-اوین-انقلاب-قطعی-است/111259/1.
12. My translation. Iran Wire, "Bahareh Hedayat from Evin Prison."
13. My translation. Iran Wire, "Bahareh Hedayat from Evin Prison."
14. See Djavad Salehi-Isfahani, "Iran: Poverty and Inequality since the Revolution," Brookings Institution, January 29, 2009, https://www.brookings.edu/opinions/iran-poverty-and-inequality-since-the-revolution/.
15. See Southern Poverty Law Center, "Anti-Muslim," https://www.splcenter.org/fighting-hate/extremist-files/ideology/anti-muslim.
16. See Aliah Abdo, "The Legal Status of Hijab in the United States: A Look at the Sociopolitical Influences on the Legal Right to Wear the Muslim Headscarf," UC Law San Francisco, October 2, 2018, https://repository.uclawsf.edu/hastings_race_poverty_law_journal/vol5/iss2/6/.
17. I made an earlier version of this argument in a short essay, "How Iranian Women's Bodies Became an Ideological Battleground," *Middle East Eye*, September 28, 2022, https://www.middleeasteye.net/opinion/iran-women-bodies-became-ideological-battleground.
18. For more details, see Catherine Shoard, "Jafar Panahi Sentenced to Six Years in Jail," *The Guardian*, July 19, 2022, https://www.theguardian.com/film/2022/jul/19/jafar-panahi-sentenced-to-six-years-in-jail.
19. For more details on the centrality of women in Beizai's cinema, see Hamid Dabashi, "Bahram Bezai: Bashu, The Little Stranger," in *Masters and Masterpieces of Iranian Cinema* (Washington, DC: Mage, 2007), 253–78.

20. See Dabashi, *Masters and Masterpieces*, 370–92.

21. For more on intersectionality, see Columbia Law School, "Kimberlé Crenshaw on Intersectionality, More than Two Decades Later," June 8, 2017, https://www.law.columbia.edu/news/archive/kimberle-crenshaw-intersectionality-more-two-decades-later.

22. Similar themes were first explored by another Iranian filmmaker, Ali Zhakan, years earlier in *Madian* (The Mare), in 1985.

23. An earlier version of this reflection on Iranian cinema and the Zhina uprising appeared as "Women, Life, Freedom: How Iran Protests Were Foretold in Film," *Middle East Eye*, December 16, 2022, https://www.middleeasteye.net/opinion/iran-protests-women-life-freedom-film-foretold-how.

TWO: THE NEXT IRANIAN REVOLUTION WILL NOT BE THEORIZED

Shirin Kamangar, "Naqd-e Birahmaneh Khizesh Tudeh-i Ari, Amma Cheguneh?" (Brutal Criticism of the Mass Uprising Yes, But How?), *Naqd*, March 2023, https://naghd.com/2023/03/23/نقد-جریان‌های-توده‌وار-شزیی‌خ-توده‌های-آری./. My translation of the original Persian.

1. Kamangar, "Naqd-e Birahmaneh."

2. Robert F. Worth, "In Iran, Raw Fury Is in the Air," *Atlantic*, October 1, 2022, https://www.theatlantic.com/ideas/archive/2022/10/iran-protests-mahsa-amini/671616/.

3. Hamid Dabashi, *The Emperor Is Naked: On the Inevitable Demise of the Nation-State* (London: Pluto, 2020).

4. Bita Malakuti, "Ma Hameh Sharik-e Jorm Hastim: Roman-e Siasi Kiumars Pourahmad dar Naqd-e Enqelab-e Islami" (We Are All Accomplices: Kiumars Pourahmad's Political Novel against the Islamic Revolution), BBC Persian, April 13, 2023, https://www.bbc.com/persian/articles/c04vr75ml1mo.

5. Slavoj Žižek, "From Democracy to Divine Violence," in *Democracy in What State?*, Giorgio Agamben et al., eds. (New York: Columbia University Press, 2011), 120.

6. I extend some of these observations in "On Syria: Where the Left Is Right and the Right Is Wrong," Al Jazeera, February 28, 2012, https://www.aljazeera.com/opinions/2012/2/28/on-syria-where-the-left-is-right-and-the-right-is-wrong.

7. Mirsepassi, *Iran's Quiet Revolution*, 1.

8. Mirsepassi, *Iran's Quiet Revolution*, 1.
9. Mirsepassi, *Iran's Quiet Revolution*, 1.
10. See Ernst Cassirer, *The Myth of the State* (New Haven, CT: Yale University Press, 1946).

THREE: THE REAL PERILS AND THE FALSE PROMISES OF ETHNIC NATIONALISM

Sherko Bekas, "Answer," was originally written in 1988. See "Three Poems," trans. Alana Marie Levinson-LaBrosse and Halo Fariq, *World Literature Today*, July 2018, https://www.worldliteraturetoday.org/2018/july/three-poems-sherko-bekas. "Translators' note: On March 16, 1988, as part of Anfal, Saddam Hussein's military campaign against the Kurds of Iraq, Halabja withstood a chemical-weapons attack. The largest directed against a civilian population in history, it has been recognized as an act of genocide by the Iraqi High Criminal Court."

1. For an earlier iteration of this part of the chapter, see Hamid Dabashi, "On the Kurdish Question," Al Jazeera, November 27, 2017, https://www.aljazeera.com/opinions/2017/11/27/on-the-kurdish-question.

2. See David M. Halbfinger, "Israel Endorsed Kurdish Independence: Saladin Would Have Been Proud," *Haaretz*, September 25, 2017, https://www.haaretz.com/2017-09-25/ty-article/israel-endorsed-kurdish-independence-saladin-would-have-been-proud/0000017f-e11e-d75c-a7ff-fd9f4b360000. Here is a key passage connecting Kurdish separatism to Israel: "And while Kurdish leaders have not publicly embraced Israel in the run-up to the referendum, for fear of antagonizing the Arab world, the Israeli flag can routinely be seen at Kurdish rallies in Erbil and across Europe." This brand of Kurdish ethnic nationalism now finds itself in complete ideological alliance with the Zionist ethnic nationalism. For a recent example of this pathological brand of Kurdish ethnic nationalism see Ahmad Mohammadpour, "The Invention of Iran: From 'Iranianness' to 'Persianness.'" *Asian Studies Review* (2024): 1–21.

3. For a detailed account of the idea of agonistic pluralism see Chantal Mouffe, *Agonistics: Thinking the World Politically* (London: Verso, 2013).

4. Mouffe, *Agonistics*, xii.

5. I have detailed these biographical accounts of my early childhood in southern Iran in *An Iranian Childhood: Rethinking History and Memory* (Cambridge: Cambridge University Press, 2023).

6. Partha Chatterjee, *The Nation and Its Fragments: Colonial and Post-*

colonial Histories (Princeton, NJ: Princeton University Press, 1993), 5. See also Benedict Anderson, *Imagined Communities: Reflections on the Origin and Spread of Nationalism* (London: Verso, 1983).

FOUR: KHIZESH AS INTIFADA AT LARGE

Ghazaleh Alizadeh, *Khaneh Idrisi-ha (The House of the Idrisis)* (Tehran: Tus Publications, 1991), 7. My translation from the original Persian.

1. They are in chronological order: *The Fox and the Paradox: Iran, the Green Movement and the USA* (2010), *Brown Skin, White Masks* (2011), *The Arab Spring: The End of Postcolonialism* (2012), *Can Non-Europeans Think?* (2015), *Europe and Its Shadows: Coloniality after Empire* (2019), and *The Emperor is Naked: The Inevitable Demise of the Nation-State* (2020).

2. Alizadeh, *Khaneh Idrisi-ha*, 2.

3. For extensive discussions of Gianni Vattimo's idea of *il pensiero debole*, see Gianni Vattimo and Pier Aldo Rovatti, eds., *Weak Thought*, trans. Peter Carravetta (Albany, NY: SUNY Press, 2012).

4. Vattimo and Rovatti, 43.

5. Vattimo and Rovatti, 45.

6. Vattimo and Rovatti, 45.

7. For main samples of their works, see V. Y. Mudimbe, *The Invention of Africa: Gnosis, Philosophy, and the Order of Knowledge* (Bloomington: Indiana University Press, 1988); Enrique Dussel, *Philosophy of Liberation*, trans. Aquila Martinez and Christine Morkovsky (Maryknoll, NY: Orbis Books, 1977/1985); and Kojin Karatani, *Isonomia the Origins of Philosophy*, trans. Joseph A. Murphy (Durham, NC: Duke University Press, 2017).

8. Hamid Dabashi, "The Third Intifada Has Already Begun," Al Jazeera, October 11, 2011, https://www.aljazeera.com/opinions/2011/10/11/the-third-intifada-has-already-begun.

9. Khosrow Parsa, "Savari Nahamvar bar Tark-e Do Asb-e Baldar" (A Rough Rider on the Back of Two Winged Horses), *Naqd-e Eqtesad-e Siasi*, May 23, 2023, https://pecritique.com/2023/05/23/سوواری-ناهموار-بر-ترک-دو-اسب-بالدار-خسر/.

10. See Homa Katouzian, "Iran's Long History and Short-Term Society," *International Journal of Political Economy* 1, no. 1 (January 2020): 23–34.

11. The main proponent of this deeply Orientalist reading of Iran as a non-European society is the British-trained student of Iranian

history Homa Katouzian. See, for example, his typical take in this regard, "The Short-Term Society: A Comparative Study in Problems of Long-Term Political and Economic Development in Iran," *International Journal of New Political Economy* 2, no. 2 (October 2021): 1–29, https://jep.sbu.ac.ir/article_101180.html. The Persian translation for "short-term society," which he has provided as "Jame'eh-ye Kolangi" (lit. "Pickaxe Society"), is a better indication of its Orientalist genealogy. "Kolangi" is a slang expression in Persian referring to a dilapidated building that is beyond saving and must be demolished and rebuilt. This is his perception of his own homeland before he immigrated to England. Trained and educated in the United Kingdom from a very early age, Katouzian openly carries many racist clichés of British colonial attitudes toward "the natives" (though he is one of those natives) in his habitually choppy, incoherent, and amateurish writings on Iranian society and culture. His entire body of work is, alas, a sad and pathological specimen of a deeply colonized mind carrying the prose and politics of the British colonialists in a consistently gauche and maladroit writing career.

12. See Jason Brennan, *Against Democracy* (Princeton, NJ: Princeton University Press, 2016).

13. James Jackson, "What's Up with Germany's Pro-Israel 'Left'?" Novara Media, December 11, 2023, https://novaramedia. com/2023/12/11/whats-up-with-germanys-pro-israel-left/.

14. Alexis de Tocqueville, *Democracy in America*, ed. Eduardo Nolla and trans. James T. Schleifer (Indianapolis, IN: Liberty Fund), vol. 1, 418.

15. For details, see Sonam Sheth, "Trump's Former National Security Advisor Says the President Should Impose Martial Law to Force New Elections in Battleground States," *Business Insider*, December 18, 2020, https://www.businessinsider.com/michael-flynn-trump-military-martial-law-overturn-election-2020-12.

16. See Hamid Dabashi, *The End of Two Illusions: Islam after the West* (Oakland: California University Press, 2022).

17. For details of Biden's victory, see the statistics of the Pew Research Center: Ruth Igielnik, Scott Keeter, and Hannah Hartig, "Behind Biden's 2020 Victory," Pew Research Center, June 30, 2021, https://www. pewresearch.org/politics/2021/06/30/behind-bidens-2020-victory/.

18. In my *Corpus Anarchicum: Political Protest, Suicidal Violence, and the Making of the Posthuman Body* (New York: Palgrave, 2012), I first explored the full dimensions of the posthuman body as the ground zero of a posthuman consciousness.

19. Rosi Braidotti, *The Posthuman* (Cambridge: Polity, 2013), 15.
20. Braidotti, *The Posthuman.*
21. Braidotti, *The Posthuman*, 50.
22. See Alizadeh, *Khaneh Idrisi-ha.* For the English translation of her other major novel, see Ghazaleh Alizadeh, *The Nights of Tehran*, trans. Mohamad Reza Ghanoonparvar (New York: Bibliotheca Iranica: Persian Fiction in Translation, 2021).
23. Alizadeh, *Khaneh Idrisi-ha*, 608.
24. Alizadeh, *Khaneh Idrisi-ha*, 611.

FIVE: DO IRANIAN WOMEN NEED SAVING?

Aghil Daghagheleh, "Foru-dasti va Lahzeh Enqelabi-ye Zhina" (Subalternity and the Revolutionary Moment of Zhina), *Naqd-e Eqtesad-e Siasi*, March 2, 2023, https://pecritique. com/2023/03/02/فرودستی-و-لحظهی-انقلابی-ژینا-عقیل-دغ-. English translation from the Persian original is mine.

1. The original Persian essay: Noushin Ahmadi Khorasani, "Hijab-e Ejbari, Qiyam Zhina, and Tabagheh-ye Motevasset" (Mandatory Veiling, Zhina Uprising, and the Middle Class), Iran Transition Council, https://iran-tc.com/2023/05/08/حجاب-اجباری-جنبش-ژینا-و-طبقهی-متوسط. All translations from this essay are mine. The essay is not dated, but it should be around fall 2022, when the uprising had just started.
2. Lila Abu-Lughod, *Do Muslim Women Need Saving?* (Cambridge, MA: Harvard University Press, 2015).
3. Lila Abu-Lughod, "Do Muslim Women Need Saving?" *American Anthropologist* 104, no. 3 (2002): 783–90.
4. See the classical argument of Talal Asad, *Anthropology and the Colonial Encounter* (New York: Humanities Press, 1973).
5. See Deepa Parent and Ghoncheh Habibiazad, "Iranian Forces Shooting at Faces and Genitals of Female Protesters, Medics Say," *The Guardian*, December 8, 2022, https://www.theguardian.com/global-development/2022/dec/08/iranian-forces-shooting-at-faces-and-genitals-of-female-protesters-medics-say.
6. Parent and Habibiazad, "Iranian Forces Shooting."
7. For more details, see Amnesty International, "Iran: Authorities Covering Up Their Crimes of Child Killings by Coercing Families into Silence," December 9, 2022, https://www.amnesty.org/en/latest/news/2022/12/iran-authorities-covering-up-their-crimes-of-child-killings-by-coercing-families-into-silence/.

8. Amnesty International, "Iran: Authorities Covering Up Their Crimes."
9. See Hamid Dabashi, *Iran, the Green Movement, and the USA: The Fox and the Paradox* (London: Zed Books, 2010).
10. I have addressed this post-Western paradigm in detail in Dabashi, *The End of Two Illusions*.
11. Frantz Fanon, "Algeria Unveiled," in *A Dying Colonialism* (New York: Grove Press, 1994), 35–68.
12. Hamid Dabashi, *The Arab Spring: The End of Postcolonialism* (London: Zed Books, 2012); and Hamid Dabashi, *The Emperor Is Naked: On the Inevitable Demise of the Nation-State* (London: Pluto, 2020).
13. Hamid Dabashi, *The Last Muslim Intellectual: The Life and Legacy of Jalal Al-e Ahmad* (Edinburgh: Edinburgh University Press, 2020).
14. For a pioneering work of solid scholarship on the matter, see Parvin Paidar, *Women and the Political Process in Twentieth-Century Iran* (Cambridge: Cambridge University Press, 1997).
15. Ziba Mirhosseini et al., eds., *Gender and Equality in Muslim Family Law: Justice and Ethics in the Islamic Legal Tradition* (London: I. B. Tauris, 2013).
16. See Aghil Daghagheleh, "Foru-dasti va Lahzeh Enqelabi-ye Zhina." I have briefly addressed the condition of subalternity in Iranian protests on an earlier occasion in Iran. See Hamid Dabashi, "Can the Subaltern Speak English?" Al Jazeera, January 18, 2018, https://www.aljazeera.com/opinions/2018/1/18/can-the-subaltern-speak-english.
17. For more, see the website of Aghil Daghagheleh: https://adagha.com.
18. Daghagheleh, "Foru-dasti va Lahzeh Enqelabi-ye Zhina." My translation from the Persian original.
19. The conditions of homoeroticism in Iranian and Persian contexts is a more complicated and detailed matter that needs further investigation of the sort that Joseph Massad has done in the Arab context in his widely discussed book, *Desiring Arabs* (Chicago, IL: University of Chicago Press, 2007).
20. Human Rights Watch, "Iran: Discrimination and Violence against Sexual Minorities," December 15, 2010, https://www.hrw.org/news/2010/12/15/iran-discrimination-and-violence-against-sexual-minorities.
21. Human Rights Watch, "Iran: Discrimination and Violence."

SIX: "CROWD IS UNTRUTH"

Søren Kierkegaard, *On the Dedication to "That Single Individual,"* trans. Charles K. Bellinger (Grand Rapids, MI: Christian Classics Ethereal Library). Available in the public domain and online: https://www.ccel.org/ccel/k/kierkegaard/untruth/cache/untruth.pdf.

1. For more details on Masih Alinejad, see the panegyric prose to be found in Astha Rajvanshi, "Iranian Dissident Masih Alinejad Won't Be Silenced," *Time*, March 2, 2023, https://time.com/6259111/masih-alinejad/. On Alinejad's Korean counterpart, see Will Sommer, "A North Korean Defector Captivated US Media. Some Question Her Story," *Washington Post*, July 16, 2023, https://www.washingtonpost.com/media/2023/07/16/yeonmi-park-conservative-defector-stories-questioned/.

2. See Benjamin Weiser, "Iranian Operatives Planned to Kidnap a Brooklyn Author, Prosecutors Say," *New York Times*, July 13, 2021, https://www.nytimes.com/2021/07/13/nyregion/iran-masih-alinejad-kidnapping.html#:~:text=The%20indictment%20describes%20a%20plot,photograph%20and%20video%20record%20Ms.

3. MEE Staff, "US Court Mandates Iran to Pay US-Based Activist $3.3m in Damages," *Middle East Eye*, July 10, 2023, https://www.middleeasteye.net/news/us-court-mandates-iran-pay-activists-family-3-million-damages.

4. MEE Staff, "US Court Mandates."

5. CNN Wire Staff, "Report: Egyptian Dad Names Child 'Facebook,'" CNN, February 21, 2011, http://www.cnn.com/2011/WORLD/meast/02/21/egypt.child.facebook/index.html#:~:text=(CNN)%20%2D%2D%20A%20man%20in,according%20to%20a%20new%20report.

6. Jane Mayer, "How Russia Helped Swing the Election for Trump," *New Yorker*, September 24, 2018, https://www.newyorker.com/magazine/2018/10/01/how-russia-helped-to-swing-the-election-for-trump.

7. Evgeny Morozov, *Net Delusion: The Dark Side of Internet Freedom* (New York: Public Affairs, 2012), 117.

8. Dexter Filkins, "The Exiled Dissident Fuelling the Hijab Protests in Iran," *New Yorker*, September 24, 2022, https://www.newyorker.com/news/daily-comment/the-exiled-dissident-fuelling-the-hijab-protests-in-iran.

9. For more details on this case of a pro-monarchist venue based outside Iran, see Maryam Sinaiee, "Iranians Welcome Joint New Year Message By Opposition Figures," *Iran International*, January 1, 2023, https://www.iranintl.com/en/202301015279.

10. Theodor W. Adorno, *The Culture Industry: Selected Essays on Mass*

Culture, ed. J. M. Bernstein (London: Routledge, 1991).

11. See Abolfazl Hajizadegan, "Instagram-e Irani dar Lahzeh Mahsa" (Iranian Instagram at the Moment of Mahsa), *Mashq-e No*, December 15, 2022, https://mashghenow.com/?p=5780.

12. Jean Baudrillard, *Simulacra and Simulation*, trans. Sheila Faria Glaser (Ann Arbor: University of Michigan Press, 1994), 3.

13. See Shoshana Zuboff, "The Coup We Are Not Talking About: We Can Have Democracy, or We Can Have a Surveillance Society, But We Cannot Have Both," *New York Times*, January 29, 2021, https://www.nytimes.com/2021/01/29/opinion/sunday/facebook-surveillance-society-technology.html. Based on this essay, I had extended its argument to the larger issue of "Orientalism" in, or reading of, distant realities. See Hamid Dabashi, "The 'Shadow Coup': Rereading Edward Said's Orientalism after Capitol Riots," *Middle East Eye*, February 23, 2021, https://www.middleeasteye.net/opinion/us-capitol-riots-coup-rereading-edward-said-orientalism.

14. Zuboff, "The Coup We Are Not Talking About."

15. See Gabriel Rockhill, "The CIA Reads French Theory: On the Intellectual Labor of Dismantling the Cultural Left," *Los Angeles Review of Books*, February 28, 2017, https://thephilosophicalsalon.com/the-cia-reads-french-theory-on-the-intellectual-labor-of-dismantling-the-cultural-left/.

16. See Elia Zureik, David Lyon, Yasmeen Abu-Laban, eds., *Surveillance and Control in Israel/Palestine: Population, Territory and Power* (London: Routledge, 2011).

17. Zuboff, "The Coup We Are Not Talking About."

18. Georg Simmel, *Conflict and the Web of Group-Affiliations* (New York: Free Press, 1955), 138–40. For further scholarship on Simmel's pioneering work, see Mary Chayko, "The First Web Theorist? Georg Simmel and the Legacy of 'The Web of Group-Affiliations,'" *Information, Communication & Society* 18, no. 12 (2015): 1419–25.

19. Hamid Dabashi, *Persophilia: The Persian Culture on the Global Scene* (Cambridge, MA: Harvard University Press, 2015), 1–29.

20. William Kornhauser, *The Politics of Mass Society* (London: Routledge, 2008/1959).

SEVEN: RETURN OF THE PAHLAVIS WITH A VENGEANCE

The opening dialogue of Bahman Farmanara's *Shazdeh Ehtejab* (*Prince Ehtejab*) (1974) is based on Houshang Golshiri's novella of the same title. For an English translation, see Houshang Golshiri, *The Prince*, trans. James Buchan (New York: Random House, 2007). The transcription and translation of the original dialogue in Persian are mine.

1. See "Nameh Bahareh Soleimani az Evin" (The Letter of Bahareh Soleimani from Evin), Radio Zamaneh, January 23, 2023, https://www.radiozamaneh.com/750732/. Translation from the original Persian letter is mine.

2. "Nameh Bahareh Soleimani az Evin."

3. For a cogent and critical reading of the consequences of Reza Pahlavi's visit to Israel, see Sarah Ariyan Sakha, "Why Pahlavi's Israel Visit Betrays Both Iranians and Palestinians," +972 *Magazine*, April 27, 2023, https://www.972mag.com/reza-pahlavi-israel-iran/. "The Abraham Accords serve as the dangerous inspiration and impetus for the Cyrus Accords that Pahlavi mentioned in his press release. Such normalization would be devastating for Iranians and Palestinians alike: it would likely bring further exports of Israeli surveillance technology and tactics to Iran, and potentially further bolster Israel's ability to act with impunity against Palestinians." This is too far-fetched. The Islamic Republic and its Chinese partners are ahead of the Israeli game in bringing those spywares to Iran to spy on and to pacify social uprisings.

4. For an eyewitness account of a visceral reaction by a former political prisoner to the appearance of the notorious SAVAK official Parviz Sabeti in pro-Pahlavi rallies, see Brian Osgood, "Divisions Roil Iranian-American Protest Movement," Al Jazeera, March 2, 2023, https://www.aljazeera.com/news/2023/3/2/hld-divisions-roil-iranian-american-protest-movement.

5. Osgood, "Divisions Roil."

6. For the most recent scholarship on the CIA-MI6 coup of 1953, see Ervand Abrahamian, *The Coup: 1953, the CIA, and the Roots of Modern US-Iranian Relations* (New York: The New Press, 2015).

7. For a detailed account of the rise of Reza Shah, see Cyrus Ghani, *Iran and the Rise of the Reza Shah: From Qajar Collapse to Pahlavi Power* (London: I. B. Tauris, 2001).

8. Karl Marx, *Capital: A Critique of Political Economy: The Process of Production of Capital*, vol. 1, book 1, trans. Samuel Moore and Edward Aveling (Moscow: Progress Publishers, n.d.). Available in the public domain: https://www.marxists.org/archive/marx/works/download/pdf/Capital-Volume-I.pdf.

9. For a photo of the billboard selling Googoosh's "Zan, Zendegi, Azadi" perfume, see "Capitalizing on the Revolution Is Disgusting Behavior," Reddit post by user faloodehx, https://www.reddit. com/r/NewIran/comments/1266k6i/capitalizing_on_the_revolution_is_disgusting/. For the picture of Golshifteh Farahani Zar Amir Ebrahimi on the cover of *Télérama*, see here: "'This Is Not a Riot. It's a Revolution,'" Reddit post by user Alef_In_Wonderland, https://www.reddit.com/r/NewIran/comments/yvk2k0/this_is_ not_a_riot_its_a_revolution_golshifteh/.

10. It is crucial to note that fetishization of the Zhina uprising by glossy magazines is radically different from the use of nude bodies as a mode of protest, as I detailed in a 2012 essay, when young women, Arab and Iranians, were using their bodies by way of protesting the political circumstances of their lives. See Hamid Dabashi, "La Vita Nuda: Baring Bodies, Bearing Witness," Al Jazeera, January 23, 2012, https://www.aljazeera.com/opinions/2012/1/23/la-vita-nu-da-baring-bodies-bearing-witness.

11. Most serious scholarship on Houshang Golshiri's work is in Persian. For a review of his work in English, see Encyclopedia Iranica, "GOLŠIRI, Hušang," https://www.iranicaonline.org/articles/gol-siri-husang. For a detailed discussion of both the original novella by Golshiri and Bahman Farmanara's film version, Dabashi, "Prince Ehtejab" in *Masters and Masterpieces of Iranian Cinema*, 167–92.

12. I have conducted an extensive interview with Bahman Farmanara detailing his collaboration with Houshang Golshiri. For this and other aspects of Farmanara's cinema see Hamdi Dabashi, *Close Up: Iranian Cinema, Past, Present, Future* (London and New York: Verso, 2001), 112–55.

13. See Hamid Dabashi, *The Persian Prince: The Rise and Resurrection of an Imperial Archetype* (Stanford, CA: Stanford University Press, 2023).

EIGHT: TOWARD A POST-ISLAMIST LIBERATION THEOLOGY

This is an actual conversation between Majid Reza Rahnavard, one of the protesters of the Zan, Zendegi, Azadi uprising, and his executioner just minutes before he was publicly hanged. Source: https://www.rouydad24.ir/fa/news/326125/وصیت-نامه-مجیدرضا-رهنورد-قبل-از-اعدام-فیلم.1. The song is available at "'Khoda Noor خدا نور' Babak Amini & Ardavan Hatami," YouTube video, posted November 28, 2022, https://www.youtube.com/watch?app=desktop&v=mQ7fgehd5wo.

2. My transcription and translation from the original Persian lyric. See "'Khoda Noor نور اخد.'"

3. Talal Asad, *Genealogies of Religion* (Baltimore, MD: Johns Hopkins University Press, 1993), 1.

4. Asad, *Genealogies of Religion*, 3–4.

5. For a brief account of my argument, see how I underlined this paradox at the center of the Islamist ideology and its failure to sustain its legitimacy in "The End of Islamic Ideology," *Social Research* 67, no. 2 (Summer 2000): 475–518.

6. See Gil Anidjar, "Secularism," *Critical Inquiry* 33, no. 1 (Autumn 2006): 59–60.

7. See Hamid Dabashi, *Being a Muslim in the World* (New York: Palgrave Pivot, 2013).

8. See Mohammad Mojtahed Shabestari, *Iman va Azadi* (Faith and Freedom) (Tehran: Tarh-e, 1376/1997).

9. Shabestari, *Iman va Azadi*, 178.

10. Shabestari, *Iman va Azadi*, 107–16.

11. Ahmad Shamlou, "Marg-e Naseri" (The Deah of the Nazarene), in *Majmu'eh Ash'ar* (Collected Poems), vol. 2 (Giessen, Germany: Bamdad Verlag, 1989), 845–48. Translation from the original Persian is mine.

CONCLUSION: CAN THE SUBALTERN SPEAK PERSIAN?

Arya Akbari, age thirteen, is a young Iranian rapper who became widely popular early in the course of the Zhina uprising, with these and other lyrics finding new significance. The video clip of this song is available online here: https://www.youtube.com/watch?v=P-BeQ-3Ull4w. Transcription of the lyrics and translation from the original Persian is mine.

1. See Hamid Dabashi, "Can the Subaltern Speak English?" Al Jazeera, January 18, 2018, https://www.aljazeera.com/opinions/2018/1/18/can-the-subaltern-speak-english.

2. See Gayatri Spivak, "Can the Subaltern Speak?" in *Marxism and the Interpretation of Culture*, eds. Cary Nelson and Lawrence Grossberg (London: Macmillan, 1988), 66–111.

3. Dabashi, "Can the Subaltern Speak English?"

4. See Hamid Dabashi, *Iran: A People Interrupted* (New York: The New Press, 2008).

5. See Arundhati Roy, *Azadi: Fascism, Fiction, and Freedom in the Time*

of the Virus (Chicago, IL: Haymarket, 2022).
6. See Agamben et. al, *Democracy in What State?*
7. See Mouffe, *Agonistics.*

INDEX

Page numbers followed by n denote notes.

231

ABOUT THE AUTHOR

Hamid Dabashi is the Hagop Kevorkian Professor of Iranian Studies and Comparative Literature at Columbia University. He received a dual Ph.D. in Sociology of Culture and Islamic Studies from the University of Pennsylvania in 1984, followed by a post-doctoral fellowship at Harvard University. Dabashi has written more than two dozen books, edited four, and contributed chapters to many more. Among his most recent books are *The Shahnameh: The Persian Epic as World Literature* (Columbia, 2019); *On Edward Said: Remembrance of Things Past* (Haymarket, 2020); and *The End of Two Illusions: Islam after the West* (University of California Press, 2022). He is the author of over one hundred essays, articles, and book reviews on subjects ranging from Iranian and Islamic studies, comparative literature, world cinema, and the philosophy of art. His books and articles have been translated into numerous languages, including Japanese, German, French, Spanish, Russian, Hebrew, Arabic, and Persian.